About the Author

Ambika Wauters writes about healing. Her work includes the realm of angels, colour and sound healing, and homeopathy. She is a practising homoeopath, workshop facilitator, principal of The School of Spiritual Homeopathy and The Institute of Life Energy Medicine. She founded The Heart of Peace Institute for children with autism and developmental delay which is a non-profit organization bringing healing to challenged children around the world. Ambika is the author of numerous successful books on angels and homeopathy including *The Homeopathic Bible* and *Angel Blessings for Babies*.

The Healing Power of Angels

How They Guide & Protect Us

AMBIKA WAUTERS

WATKINS
Sharing Wisdom Since 1893

This edition first published in the UK and USA 2011 by
Watkins, an imprint of Watkins Media Limited
Unit 11, Shepperton House
89–93 Shepperton Road,
London N1 3DF

enquiries@watkinspublishing.com

3 5 7 9 10 8 6 4

Designed and typeset by Jerry Goldie
Printed and bound in Great Britain by TJ International Ltd

A CIP record for this book is available from
the British Library

ISBN: 978-1-90748-642-5

www.watkinspublishing.com

This book is dedicated to my parents, William Israel Gerelick and Joyce Ferer Gerelick. My father taught me to work hard and love life. He gave me the moral underpinnings of my being and wonderful physical stamina. My mother brought spirit and intelligence to me and a great love of angels from an early age.

To my two sisters, Lynn Gerelick Bleecker, a gifted artist, now in spirit, and Nita Gerelick Steinberg, who has become a light in my life. To my beautiful niece, Jamie Amelia Steinberg, who brings so much love to the table.

To Nina Norell, gifted mystic, healer and teacher, whose love, support and emotional nourishment have kept me open through many initiations into the truth of love. I am deeply grateful.

Angels are with everyone
and lead us and provide that
whatever befalls us
shall turn to our good.
(Anon)

CONTENTS

Preface

This book has the capacity to connect you with the healing power of angels. Let it open your hearts and minds to this realm of possibility. It will bring you much joy in doing so. It offers you a practical, working model for engaging the angelic world for healing and rejuvenating. They can assist you with those things that have matter and significance to you through the power of their being and the love they generate to humanity.

The Healing Power of Angels describes how angels interface with us, stimulating and healing us as they work within our energy system. Our task is to speak to them through prayer, in meditation, with affirmative statements of intent and through reflection. They always respond, and as aspects of our own divinity, they link us directly with God, the living Source within us.

The angelic realm is made of nine unique layers of differentiated beings which are known as levels of divinity. These beings are categorized by their proximity to the Throne of God. Starting at the lowest level, which is closest to humanity, and moving higher towards the Throne of God, they are: Angels, Archangels, Archai, Dynamis, Dominions, Virtues, Seraphim, Cherubim and Thrones.

These degrees of differentiation in the angelic world exist in three levels of heaven, known as the Heaven of Form, the Heaven of Creation and the Heaven of Paradise. Each level has three types of angelic beings residing within it.

The angelic realm responds to prayer and petition. They will never interfere with us, but if we ask for help they will provide instant assistance. They contact us in stillness, through our dreams and in reflective moments. They also work within the human energy system to balance our energy field.

Angels are an integral part of us. They work within us to stimulate the chakras, or energy power centers. They influence and inform the four subtle energy bodies. As part of their mission to assist us in awakening to the truth of ourselves they also bring us love and understanding along with divine blessings and the grace of the Holy Spirit.

They support our life force by keeping us strong, healthy and moving forward in life. They act as God's agents, helping to make our lives fuller and happier. As we get to know the many ways in which they enhance the quality of our lives we become masterful in asking that our needs be met and our desires fulfilled. They are here to help us realize the truth of our spiritual perfection.

Angels "talk" to us by whispering in our ears. When we are comfortable with silence we can hear their wisdom clearly, and we are able to receive their encouragement and guidance. They want us to know the truth of ourselves, which is that we are one with all creation, never separate from it. They ask us to love ourselves, honor who we are, and, as much as possible, to follow the desires of our heart.

Angels can give us very simple and practical advice, along with spiritual guidance. They are always involved with what is going on in our daily life, from doing the laundry, paying our bills, to picking the children up from school. There is never a time they are not with us. They see us through the challenges and the joyful times.

Our job is to learn to listen carefully to their guidance and trust in their counsel. They see a far bigger picture of our lives than we will ever imagine. They work on our behalf constantly and are the trusted servants of God. They bring fulfillment and happiness to our lives.

They work deeply within our energy field to lift our spirits and balance our systems. They keep us moving forward in life till our tasks on this earth plane have been completed and our soul is ready to go home to God again. They build inner strength and moral fiber in us. They release doubt, build trust and they always, always, love us, no matter what we think or do. They help us face our destiny with courage, love, and consciousness.

The angelic realm supports our psychological growth and spiritual development. They encourage us to cultivate a real, working relationship with them. They can guide us through the obstacles that are on our path. They can help us overcome them, zigzag around them or jump over them. They take the high watch on our path through life.

The more we trust in their guidance and make it our own the better we are able to release the chronic patterns of victimhood, martyrdom and servility that have been grafted onto our consciousness by family, school and church. As we release these patterns that limit us we come into the power and truth of ourselves.

We can choose to be the receptors of this divine wisdom and guidance. The more we love ourselves, know our true value and accept the world around us as part of God, the stronger the angelic forces work in our lives.

Of course, the choice to be the repositories of this love and guidance is ours. We can think we are doing it all on our own, including suffering and struggling, or we can surrender to and acknowledge that nothing really gets done without the help of God and His angels. They are the force through which our life moves. Carolyn Myss, the great modern mystic, once said, "We couldn't tie our shoes without the help of angels!" I believe she is right.

We can work with them to co-create our lives. By cultivating our imaginative forces to see our good unfold, and trust the desires of our heart for love and success, we open a channel for angels to work with us. This relationship serves healing in all ways because a universal law says that no one heals alone.

Knowing that we have divine guidance working on our behalf at all times allows us to access this guidance at any time we need help. Angels guide and assist us in fulfilling our destiny by bringing healing directly into our lives and the lives of those around us. We are all fortified and strengthened in this relationship with them.

For us on the earth plane, who see tragedy, loss and pain, this connection with angels allows us to trust in a higher good. It takes faith to know God is always working, even though we may not always see that good unfolding.

Angels can help us find pleasure and play in the game of life. They can show us a higher truth, and see the real meaning and depth of life. They can help us release the struggle that is so easily associated with earthly life. The angels' job description is to act as our coaches and be our guides to see us through the challenging experiences and spiritual initiations of life.

The angels are readily accessible to us through meditation, prayer, affirmation and reflective practice. These are the tools that provide us with direct access to the Divine. As we cultivate these tools our relationship with angels becomes stronger. We realize we are supported, guided and carried forward by their great love and power. Each time we make a spiritual connection we become stronger, feel safer and are more assured that our good is unfolding. We are also more deeply connected to the truth of ourselves in the process of connection.

Angels strive to keep us aware of the Divine Presence. It is in this Presence that we live, breathe and have our being. Knowing we are one with God frees us from the pain of separation. This presence unites us with all life. It is in this awareness that we are held, blessed and guided by the great forces for good we know as angels.

Angels shower our being with love and let our hearts shine in radiance and beauty. They do this because they love us. They can carry our spirit beyond the abyss of grief and loss. They not only live around us, they reside within us. They fill our subtle bodies with God's love, nurturing every cell of our being.

When we allow this love to become conscious within us we align ourselves with spirit; we become attuned to the rhythms and vibrations of the universe. We become one with the pulse of universal life. This is what keeps us healthy, vibrant and youthful. It keeps us moving in the direction of growth, healing and love.

Angels inspire us to learn sacred knowledge. Within the eternal truths lie the answers to the problems that plague the world today. Finding the truth of nature, the meaning of life and the purpose of our own personal existence is revealed within the great repositories of wisdom held in the sacred texts of all religions. They live at the heart of the angelic realm. When we are ready to receive this knowledge and use it wisely it is given to us in the form of inspiration or, simply, inner knowing.

Angels offer us their protection and strive to keep us safe. They want us to feel safe in the whole universe, at home with our Creator as well as with one another. They bring us the help we need to live fully in sufficiency. They heal, bless, and support us throughout lifetimes of transformation. And, most importantly, they bring us love which we can use to heal our wounds of isolation and separation.

All that angels ask of us is that we communicate what we want and need. We must learn to trust that our prayers are answered in the best ways that suit our individual needs. Angels guarantee that we are heard, seen, and loved.

Angels want us to expand our awareness. They long to be included in our daily lives as part of the force that moves the day forward easily, effortlessly and without stress. They encourage us to see the bigger picture of our reality and incorporate that in our daily lives.

Angels want us to know we are always living in freedom, and we can choose to release blocked emotions and negative thoughts that weigh our spirit down. They pray we will forgive the hurts of the past and call in love to light up and heal the world around us.

The angels' job is to help us ascend to higher levels of consciousness. Each step takes us closer to embracing God as Source, which is the living presence within us. Each step allows us to intensify our capacity to receive love and healing. As you look back on your life, notice the expanding patterns of growth and love that have been turning points in your life.

You can acknowledge your spiritual growth as part of the simple evolutionary process of life itself. This is facilitated by the angelic spirits that work within you. They carry the responsibility for your good and the greater good of humanity as their evolutionary task.

Those moments when you chose to love, heal or tell the truth are the defining moments of your spiritual path. You may see, with your inner eye, the gentle footprints angels left on your consciousness during these times of transition and change. They helped you keep your heart open and your mind uncluttered so you could make a choice for love. They encouraged you, like a team of cheerleaders, to say yes to yourself, yes to life, yes to love!

This book offers you a way to consciously engage with the angelic realm and to form a loving, trusting and deeply abiding friendship with them. If you allow them they will help you with your health, wholeness, prosperity, relationships and whatever your heart desires. It is a guide to cultivating a wonderful and loving friendship with angels. They want to be known in your life. They want you to know them, love them and seek their help.

My Personal Connection With Angels

My connection grew out of a childhood fascination with angels. From stories, books, dolls, questions emerged and were duly answered by my mother, my religious teachers and my many Catholic friends who had a wondrous love and belief in angels. I explored this realm in dreams, and as I grew up I found people who shared a real love of angels and could explain them to me in ways I could grasp.

This path of inquiry is still expanding. It is a relationship that constantly inspires and informs my life. When I am lost, unsure, afraid or need help I call on them for guidance. "Please help me," has been a constant prayer through my adult life.

I have a sense that my spirit is strengthened and fortified by their love, guidance and protection. Nothing is lovelier or draws my attention more than the form of angels in art, and even imposed on nature. I can find angels in clouds, rock formations, and tree clusters. I see them in paintings, on dashboards of cars, and in the faces of kind people.

I require their help to see me through the day and manage the affairs of my life. I am skilled in certain areas of life and weak in others, just like most people. Where I cannot develop expertise quickly enough I require the help of angels.

They may appear as the repair men, my computer techie, Daniel, or my blessed housekeeper, Tanny. They come in the form of my gardener, Jorge, Leigh the hairdresser, the banker, teachers, priests and rabbis I know. They are my good friends, or my blessed literary agent, Susan Mears, who once brought me a poem about the Archangel Michael and suggested I read it daily for one year. All these people are angels in my life. They make my life go forward in blessing and love.

Angels are everywhere, in human and non-human form. I have learned to call on them when I am stuck, confused and need help. 'Why struggle and suffer more than I have to?' is a question I often ask. I have learned to ask for help.

Angels appear in my dreams, and are often disguised as the loving and kind people I meet daily. They help me when my world needs healing, transforming or to be shaken up. I know angels are there to see me through and stand at my side. I have learned over years to ask for help and know they will see me through. I have trained myself to listen to their true, deep guidance that instructs me with humor and precision. My life is so much easier and works so much better because of the conscious relationship we share.

There are many times in my life when I will address a prayer to them for help, for myself or for a friend, and receive assurance that all is well. I have learned to trust that inner guidance that comes at unusual moments when I am driving, at the market, walking or swimming laps. I know the ring of their lilt and the cadence of their wings around me. They always lead me to the truth and greater understanding.

Angels take me forward in my life when I am stuck and forget the truth of who I am. They never drop me, punish me or mock my plea for help, be it for love, financial assistance, health issues or relationship problems. They are as constant as life itself.

I have learned, from books and spiritual sources, that we must be willing to ask them directly for the help we need. I have found the hard part of this exercise is asking for precisely what I want, letting go and waiting for a response.

When I ask there is always an answer. They are, after all, the agents of the Divine Presence in which we all live, breathe and have our being. How could they possibly let us down. We are one in each other.

Angels have awakened me to the best experiences of my life. I have learned that when an idea persists in my mind the angels are working on my consciousness. There is definitely something I am being asked to know. These are times when I go inside, walk around my medicine wheel, in prayer and petition, sit quietly, and rest in the assurance that their guidance wants to be heard.

I can sit for weeks with this guidance working within me. I can wonder and ponder until I feel I can follow through with the messages I receive. I have been inspired to begin a program for children with autism, been led to write, travel, live in foreign countries, and meet certain people who held a piece of the puzzle of my life.

I have been led to train and qualify in homeopathy, move back to my country of origin after 28 years abroad, and I have been led to live a simple, meaningful and creative life that is fun, joyful and full of mirth. I have solved my health problems through their guidance, managed financial issues with their help and reconciled relationships with people that were challenging. I have learned to be free, keep my boundaries intact and develop a strong moral fiber with their guidance.

Perhaps the greatest gift they bring me is the love of spirit which deepens and grows as I mature. Without that in my life I would find far too many things senseless and painful. I have come to trust and have faith in the Divine Presence in all things. I know truly, within my heart, that all is well.

I have learned to love and value angelic guidance over and over again. That is why this book is something that I believe can help you find the truth of yourself and the joy you seek. If you love angels I hope this book inspires you to go deeper in your search for the truth of yourself.

I know that in moments of great confusion and uncertainty I have been led to seek higher ground through their help. I have found my way, made the necessary changes that were required of me, and come through daunting trials that could have left my spirit damaged and bruised. Thanks to the spiritual guidance I received, and paid attention to, they did nothing but nudge me ahead on my path.

They have always brought me the higher truths that helped me expand my consciousness. I have always been safe and protected in the process. They always saw me through. I am deeply grateful for the power of their healing and the grace of their love. I feel this is for anyone who seeks the connection with angels.

Angels have opened the doors of my mind and heart over these many years of working as a healer and writer. Through daily meditation I have come to experience their encouragement, feel their support and know their love. Their healing is constant and available whenever I ask for it.

They have guided me through many experiences that have strengthened and developed me, and brought me in touch with aspects of myself that needed to be healed. They always point the way, saying, "You may wish to consider healing this idea about yourself which is not congruent with the truth of you." Ultimately, this has led me to greater experiences of my wholeness and to my highest good.

Angels have brought me inner peace and heartfelt stillness at times of frustration and agitation. Through their care I have received warmth and tenderness. I feel immense gratitude for the connection I share with them and I would like to share that with you in this book.

Angels have encouraged me to let go, release fear and anger by "whispering in my ears" that I need to move on and forgive. They have engineered people coming and going in my life to help me see myself better.

They remind me the Source is always within me and that I can choose to connect with that core or struggle and do things my way. I have learned to appreciate ease rather than "my way." They awaken me to every aspect of myself, bringing assistance when I need it and opening doors of opportunity when it is time to move forward.

My personal path of spiritual inquiry has bridged many religions over several years. My path has led me to New Thought, Science of Mind, mystical Christianity, Judaism, Hinduism, Anthroposophy, Native American shamanism, and Buddhism. Every teaching has offered a rich contribution to understanding how the spiritual mysteries unfold and how angels work in our lives.

It is interesting to me that angels are a part of every spiritual tradition. They exist in all cultures in some recognizable form. The ancient and wise sages throughout the history of humanity have known and shared their existence. I think that this is because they are not foreign to us, but an intrinsic aspect of our being.

Working With Angels

The relationship with angels is a gift available to everyone. Angels can help you find what you seek, be it love and joy, financial stability, or directions when you are lost. They bring us solutions for health, love, prosperity, harmony, and joy. They help us with challenges in our relationships as well as issues around abundance. It is our choice to allow them to help us.

Tuning in to angels works best when you develop the working tools that facilitate a good, open relationship with them. Speaking "Angel" is a language of the heart and it comes directly out of your soul. We want to open our channels of communication with them so we can easily access their guidance directly and immediately. Sometimes that single word, "Help!" is all we need to say. Our prayers do not need to be complex, in a foreign language or long for them to be heard and to work.

There are tools to ask for help and tools to help us listen. Each tool teaches us to tune into ourselves. We listen when they speak to us and receive their wisdom and guidance. We learn to petition them for the help we require or that may help a friend in need. These tools keep our minds clear, our emotions stable and our spirit open. It only takes a little practice and our connections get stronger each time we make the effort.

The first tool, of course, is meditation. It provides singular moments of stillness which bring inner peace, relaxation, stability and freedom. It allows you to let down from the tensions of the day or to start your day connected with your essence.

Meditation is listening silently and carefully to the quiet, wise guidance of your soul. Meditation is a very ancient tool practiced since the beginning of man's spiritual life. It is the stillness of our mind that allows us to feel and experience the truth of our connection with God within us. It calms the mind sufficiently to bring inner stability in times of change and trouble and it releases tension, fear and anxiety. Meditation can be done for 2 to 20 minutes in the morning and at night. It need not be prescriptive but a simple time to sit quietly and recognize your Self.

The second tool is prayer. This connects us directly with Source within us. It allows us to claim our good, and acknowledge the blessings of our life in gratitude. It lets us offer up our petitions to a higher power knowing they are always heard and received.

Prayer is the language of the soul. It comes from the deepest place within us. It acknowledges our abiding connection with God as our Source. It bypasses what appear to be impossible and challenging situations and says: In God all things are possible.

The third tool we use to access our angels is affirmation. Affirmations are positive statements of intention. They help us define and express what we want and hope for in our lives. Affirmations are always said in the first person, present tense. They are always positive in intent. They align your will with the universal spirit that always says YES to you. An example of an affirmation is: "I am always open to knowing my highest good and greatest joy."

Affirmations align your will with the Law that governs the universe. The universe always gives you what you claim for yourself. If you say: "I am ugly and nobody loves me," then the universe will say "yes" and that will become your reality and experience of life. If you say: "I am beautiful and everybody loves me," the universe will say "yes" and that will become your reality and experience.

The choice is always yours to affirm. So speak it out, loudly and clearly. Make your intention to the universe very apparent by saying: I affirm the joy and beauty of my life now.

Reflective practice is the last tool and is one of the deepest ways of knowing the highest truth of your experiences. It is a way of looking carefully at a person, a group of people or a particular situation to assess what is happening at a deep level of truth. It requires stilling the mind and asking to know the truth of a situation or a person in your life. It asks that you hold the question, ponder the realm of possibilities related to your inquiry and work it through, step by step, till you arrive at a level of truth that affirms both you and others. It will help you trust your capacity for discernment, compassion and love.

Reflective practice means you are consciously considering a situation from a spiritual perspective. That means that your outcome is wholeness, love and acceptance, no matter how long that takes to form in your mind.

You ask the questions: "What is going on here? How can I know the truth of this person or this experience?" If you ponder this truth it will help in seeing the truth and allow you to honor your feelings, no matter how negative they may appear at first.

You may struggle for days, weeks, months and years to know the truth of a difficult or challenging situation. However, by applying reflective practice you work with your thoughts and feelings to arrive at the truth. You become adept at understanding the higher meaning of your experiences. You look at your attitudes, your beliefs and your projections onto other people. It is a wonderful tool for helping you release negativity and find your freedom.

The angels are always working to bring our desires into creation. They help us clear the path so that love, healing and goodness are our experience. The creative principal is known as manifestation. The angels help us manifest our deepest longings and most cherished dreams.

They work to manifest these into reality. They teach us, most of all, that we are worthy of what we say we want in life. Their job is to help the good come to us in ways that are resonant with our experience and framed within the context of our understanding.

Angels teach us how to create a richer and more beautiful life for ourselves. They show us that by affirming our worth and honoring our choices for love our life improves. Falling in love with life, accepting ourselves fully and deepening our capacity to accept our life enriches their ability to bring healing to us. They remind us love is always possible, that goodness prevails and all is well.

Your goal in this relationship with angels is to consider them when you are in trouble or need assistance. You must make room for them in your heart and mind to fully experience their healing power working within you. They long to love you and see you well.

Sometimes I fill notebooks with endless questions and ask them for answers. I will practice listening to them with my inner ear. At times I will work with a pendulum to receive a "yes" or "no" answer to my question. I trust my guidance with each passing day to know the truth and healing they bring me. You can practice ways of becoming attuned to them.

Angels want to see you steady, stable and grounded in life. They are invested with healing the earth, and not having spaced-out people dropping out of life. They need you to be attentive to your own healing and to want wellness, health and happiness.

When you become aware of their presence working in your life you will marvel at how they can help you accomplish your tasks, smile through extraordinary challenges and, most of all, find your happiness. They know that when you are happy, the world is a better place.

They love acknowledgment and gratitude as their reward. A simple "thanks" goes a long way in saying to them that you could not have accomplished this task without their help. Acknowledgment and gratitude help you say "yes" to your life as well. It reminds you how blessed you truly are. When you say "thank you" to angels you are saying "thank you" to yourself.

By seeking their help and allowing them to consciously serve you, they help you create the life you want. As you call in ease, pleasure and joy, or whatever your heart desires, thank the angels. You will enjoy their sense of delight, humor and fun as you cultivate a rich friendship with them.

When you engage with the angels you will know what it's like to have someone on your side. You will experience support for your dreams and creative efforts.

The angels' greatest gift to us is their grace. This, ultimately, brings us the healing we need to live our lives in a wholesome and positive way. Their love, warmth and joy are yours to enjoy. I hope you will allow angels to light your path so blessings may flow easily and effortlessly.

Be blessed.

Ambika Wauters,
Tucson, Arizona, 2010

Introduction

The Divine Presence is omnipresent and omnipotent. It is everywhere; at all times we are submerged in it. It is the same with our relationship with angels. There is never a moment we are outside of God's love or embrace or separate from our angels. Even though we may be challenged to believe this it is a universal truth. This knowledge of the presence of angels lives in us. It moves in and through us, as we move and breathe in it.

We are one unified field, always a part of the totality of life, never separate from it. Each person is an individual expression of that wholeness we call God. We may not always be aware of it, but this Divine Presence is always surrounding us.

The Divine Presence exists in everything. It informs our being through the endless variety of experiences that make us aware. We can experience it in moments of silence and stillness, during meditation and reflection, and we can experience it in Time Square, rush hour in Hong Kong, or any place else there is frenetic activity with abundant, teaming life. It shows up in the daily miracles we encounter in ordinary life, no matter what the conditions.

The Divine Presence lives as us, expresses itself through us and connects us with all life, visible and invisible. As we engage in our daily life we see its manifestations all around us. It shows itself in the warmth and love of people, and in the beauty of nature. It is apparent in every encounter, each experience, and in all transactions we engage in. To know the Divine Presence in ourselves is to know the truth of who we are. That is what we want to hold fast to at all times. We want to be able to anchor that truth in our selves. When we experience this truth we share that light of love, living within us, with the world.

The angelic realm brings humanity God's healing and love. We could define this presence as the non-visible aspect of God working in the material world of substance. It has degrees of differentiation, and levels of consciousness and strength.

Each degree of differentiation is a unique angelic being. It creates the spiritual events of our life. When we struggle with negativity, feel doubts, fear or confusion, we may need the help of a particular angelic being to release this brand of negativity.

The angelic realm can help us heal physical illness, increase prosperity, and bring us the good we claim for ourselves. Love, relationships, friendships, business opportunities, and energy are all within our grasp. When we call the angels to our side they help us realize that which we long for and hope to have in our lives.

It is important to remember angels are not separate from our existence, rather they are a part of us. They are working in alignment with God, the living Source within us. They actually are an extension of our being. They know the truth of us as whole, complete, and already perfect. They do not make an effort to change us but wish to see us fulfill our deepest potential for happiness and good. They are always striving to bring us that which will fulfill us.

To know the power of angels is to call forth our spiritual powers to see our lives as thriving and whole. They remind us that our spirit is a radiant reflection of the inner light. When our soul is free we are luminescent.

Yes, angels know and love the truth of us. They do not collude with our negative litany of unworthiness, nor do they punish us. They work within our consciousness to see our spirit expand, assimilate and digest new ideas, and learn new forms of being that can support our joy. They stimulate each energy center with awareness and energy.

In some spiritual traditions times are set aside each day for prayer, meditation and reflection. These moments are conscious connections with God. They remind us that the Source lives within us and is holy. Creating a spiritual practice that will align your spirit with the Great Spirit and connect you with the living presence within you is the task of all spirituality.

Making the time each day to honor your indelible connection with spirit keeps you clear. It reminds you that there is a greater power than the small, edited self controlling our lives.

Becoming grounded in our spiritual practice allows our daily lives to run smoothly, effortlessly and with ease. As we tune into the angelic realm we can seek counsel, hear answers and find solutions. We become masterful in creating our lives with their help.

The gift of consciousness is to shine its light on our ordinary, daily life. Then when we have done that we shine it onto the bigger problems that face the world. We can pray for our family, friends, communities and ourselves as well as the great global tragedies and disasters that afflict the world each day. It only takes a second to send a thought of hope and help and let the angels carry that forward. We must trust that it all works for the good.

Besides the obvious positive effects of meditation it also calms the spirit and helps the physical body discharge tension. It allows us to feel safe and relaxed, and, at the same time, connected to our center. The blessings of a daily spiritual practice fill us with the love of spirit and, like working out at the gym, or jogging, go a long way to build the spiritual muscles we need to face the challenges of life.

We become, in these moments, saturated with the Divine, connected to Source within ourselves, and able to accomplish those tasks that would have brought us to our knees without this inner strength. We find our way out of challenges and dark places because we build inner strength through prayer and meditation.

Our physical body is the channel through which we experience God. By releasing toxicity from our minds and bodies we actually come closer to feeling the Divine Presence working within us. Our life view reflects the balance of our spiritual connection: staying in touch with the truth, finding beauty around us and feeling the freedom of our spirit take us deep into the realm of love that sustains all life.

Today we are inundated with high levels of toxicity in our food, water and the environment. This limits our capacity to see, hear, and feel the presence of God expressing Itself through us. Many people pray over and bless their food and water today to help eliminate its toxicity. Their prayers purify and bless what goes into their body.

By blessing our enemies, and forgiving all hurtful experiences, we release emotional toxins. Letting go of the past lightens our spirit. It sets us free to live in the moment. Releasing old hurts, fears and doubts sets us free of negativity. It frees the spirit to shine brightly in the eternal truth of who we are.

These are ancient tools, used by mystics, saints and spiritual teachers for generations to connect the human spirit more closely in God. These tools are available to everyone and do not require training or certifications. They do, however, require a willing-ness to experience connecting with the spiritual realm.

All angels are God's agents for good. Their work is to bring mankind love and awareness, to protect the delicate balance between free will and mechanical actions. They serve mankind as great friends through our individual and collective destinies. Love permeates the universe and is everywhere, and it is the medium in which angels exist. They know no sense of separation from Source so their existence is fluid and flows with ease, and they only know joy and love.

They flow through the rhythm of our breath and the pulse of our blood. They work in the subtle bodies of our energy systems. We can experience the amazing joy they bring by simply being still for a single moment. They are always working within us, day and night, conscious or unconscious. It is always best to allow them to know you are aware and grateful for all their help.

Angels are a simple reminder that we are totally united with the mind and heart of God. We are never separate from Source. The angels are channels of the Divine truth of God.

Turning the bad into the positive takes a spiritual consciousness. That is what we strive to do in seeing the good rather than living the bad. The goodness and the manifestations of His power and love hold us steady, take us forward, and allow us to co-create our lives in Him.

When we are enmeshed in the delusion of separation and too engaged in the drama of life we forget the truth of ourselves. We diminish the connection with God, which is always there, as are His angels. We get caught up with other things that feel more important to us. We are never judged but we may sometimes need to be reminded of a higher reality. Our conscious work is to keep those connections vital and open.

We are, after all, the vessels through which God channels His love to flow into the world. We fulfill that role when we stay connected with ourselves and live in faith and trust. We are the connection through which the Holy Spirit spreads Its grace. The whole spiritual world shines through us when we are connected within ourselves.

What Are Angels?

Angels are traditionally known as agents of God's good. They also manifest in many earthly forms because God and all the angels need us to be and act as His agents from time to time. Angels can manifest as pets, friends, teachers, and even our enemies. We may fail to recognize them as the angels who brought us healing or change. It takes great spiritual power to play the enemy so that a person can become conscious of who they are and what needs healing.

Angels bring awareness, in whatever form it may manifest. They offer us love and truth in forms we need to be able to understand and accept. They manifest as anything that awakens us to the truth of our selves, and that includes forces of nature that make us reflect on the power of the unknown. Angels work through all things that have the capacity to enhance our connection with God.

We, too, become angels in other people's lives. We may not recognize the gifts we bring but, be assured, we act as channels for others' higher good. God asks us to inspire, help, love and support His creatures in all ways. Sometimes we do this knowingly and at other times we are surprised to find we are those agents that bring about change and consciousness. We are simply in the right place at the right time to be of assistance and support.

Sometimes healing comes from listening carefully and attentively to a person who is struggling and suffering. At other times we may simply offer a smile, share a greeting or give a hug before we move on our way. There are times in our lives we will know the angel who opens our heart, and, hopefully, we will be grateful for the role he or she played in bringing us one step further along our path.

Angels always help us see a bigger and brighter picture of love and healing. We know to be ever thankful to them for the gift they bring. At other times, the angels are less obvious to us. We may need time to reflect long and hard on the changes that have occurred in our lives. Angels can be anyone who serves our awakening, in any form, to the truth of God working in our lives.

We may not see the gifts they brought us for years to come or even recognize them in this lifetime. Angels can appear at any time and in any form that reminds us we are loved – cherished, in fact – by the Creator. They may remind us we, too, have a destiny to fulfill and that we are in need of healing.

Angels can work through complex technology to serve us. They can arrange a friendly call from a friend or family member when we are lonely and unsure of ourselves. They can come in the form of wonderful movies, good books, or a radio program that is informative and enlightening. They can come in an email from someone offering good tidings and wonderful news. Our job is to stay open to the realm of possibility that the good is coming. Our job is to be discerning and neutral.

To be an angel you need only be willing to open your heart to sharing the love you carry within you. We can all be angels if we choose to be. Take a moment to claim your blessings now.

Honor yourself as a source of love and be an angel in someone's life. You don't need to make a grand gesture; sometimes a smile or a hug is enough to help someone feel they are seen as well as considered. Remember that now is the time for healing and reconciliation. You are a part of the transformation taking place on planet earth right now. That qualifies you for angelhood.

PART 1

WORKING WITH THE ANGELS FOR GROWTH AND DEVELOPMENT

INTRODUCTION

Angels offer us the opportunity to interface with the Divine Presence in how we see our lives. We will find that each time we petition for a happier, healthier and more joyful life we are led to a deeper belief in the power of prayer, and the efficacy of the spiritual world to honor our needs. As we come to trust more and more in the goodness of life, our place in the universe gets anchored in the truth of our being; we are children of God and we welcome all the good available to us. Growth and development are essential for our spiritual evolution. We honor what is good, whole and loving in us and we focus our intentions on expanding our levels of ease, prosperity and pleasure. God wants us happy and angels are those dear agents who help provide that for us through their ability to manifest our intentions.

The tools in this section of the book are designed to refine your skills in meeting your angels directly. As you become comfortable with meditation, prayer and reflection you naturally will affirm your right to goodness. Take your time in developing these skills, and do not punish yourself if you forget to practice them. They are a natural part of your spirit and you will eventually settle into them with ease and grace. Be blessed in your experiences and know they are all for your healing.

CHAPTER 1

How the Angels Work Within Us

Angels work within us by stimulating, toning and balancing our energy field. This field is the extension of our physical body that emanates from our core as subtle energy bodies. All of these bodies are contained in the envelope we call the auric field. It is comprised of fine particles of light and has a very subtle radiance. Some can see it and others can feel it emanating off of a person as a vibration or feeling of warmth.

The aura contains four main bodies of energy, in degrees of refinement from one another. These bodies are known as our physical body, our energy body, our spiritual body and our soul body. These are the four main bodies we carry within the aura. Other finer bodies are not mentioned here because of the complex nature of their importance in our healing.

What is essential to know is that our energy field and the angelic realm are indelibly interconnected. We live in a unified field where there is no separation from God, His angels and all of life, so therefore the angelic realm cannot exist separate from us.

Angels align themselves within our field, working through our chakra centers. They create a resonance that connects them with all other individual fields at a very high vibration. It is a delusion to think we are separate and distinct, when, in fact, there is only a unified field of creation in which we all live, breathe and have our being. What we do have is our own individual pattern of expression, known as who we are, that is the unique manifestation of God.

We are compelled in our quest to know the truth of both these laws. With the awareness that we are one there is also the awareness that we are an individual expression of that oneness. This is the highest truth of our being. Each individual is connected to a large web of energy that connects us all to this earth, the solar system and the universe.

Angels work within our individual body, our family body, our community body, our national body, our global body and even our universal body. There are angels that hold the forces of the earth together and those that bring us the great cosmic pulse of love that beats through the universe as God's love and Presence.

The angelic realm, working within our being, helps transform our small, edited individuality into a higher vibration of truth and love that connects us more fully with the whole. As they work within us we become increasingly more connected with all of life. We express who we are with greater clarity, more feeling, and a deeper spiritual resonance.

This awareness allows angels to work together with us towards developing a mastery of consciousness that nourishes life and sets the stage for everyone to come to the table of love. This helps us purify our spirit and, at the same time, it strengthens the oneness that we are all connected to.

This connection, when awakened, heals our bodies and recalibrates our subtle energies in alignment with the universal frequencies. This helps us vibrate in the same harmonics, share common dreams and express ourselves knowing we are safe and understood. All this helps align our field towards an enduring and real cosmic harmony.

Healing happens when we integrate our individual presence with the great cosmic rhythms that carry the vibrations of love and goodness to all life. It happens very quickly. One minute we experience ourselves as separate and then we awaken to the truth that this is not so. We know we are connected to every living being that exists. We share the same ideas of wholeness, longing for love, desire for health, prosperity and creativity.

These rhythms bring powerful waves of grace to us. Our work is to allow ourselves to receive them. We do this by simply allowing it into our lives. Again the power of meditation is to allow us to receive our good.

These great waves of love and truth inundate the earth all the time, but are particularly strong at the times of year when the seasons change or when there is an auspicious festival. Holidays such as the Holy Nights of Christmas, Easter week, Yom Kippur and the Jewish High Holy Days, and other religious holidays such as Ramadan remind us that millions of people are turning their attention to God and celebrating their oneness with spirit. These can be intense times of consciousness when the veil between the material world and the spirit realm is thin. It is in these times that we experience the deep connection with God and we align our consciousness more closely with Source.

Angels work within our individual being to help facilitate the healthy flow of life for the duration of our time on earth. The quality of our life is dependent on our free choice. We can live in negativity and despair or we can choose life in all its glory. It is not dependent on external factors, but on our choice as to how we wish to experience our life.

Angels can expand our consciousness by nourishing our

hearts and minds with new ideas, opening us to joy, bringing us the gifts of peace and love that we hunger for. They can help stabilize our inner resources to enable us to release the old and receive our good through wonderful experiences that honor our choices for love.

Spiritual experiences need time to be digested and assimilated, and work their way into our growing consciousness. They are designed by angels to help us realize that we are loved, cared for and guided. They help us meet our need for connection and they teach us to enjoy even frivolous encounters. They encourage us to greet strangers, make new friends, find work and projects that resonate with our heart forces. Life is designed in such a way as to teach us to love ourselves and create our good.

The angelic realm channels the universal life force to us in many forms. It may come to us as love, healing, and consciousness. This force moves, like the great cosmic dance it is, weaving through our being, permeating our cells, healing our bodies, and expanding our hearts and minds. It fortifies our soul.

This flowing cosmic rhythm has a pulse that supplies us with physical energy, emotional awareness, lucid thoughts, and, above all, spiritual consciousness.

We may not perceive these waves in our everyday existence but if we tap into what is going on around us we will feel the truth of this rhythm. It is intent and focused underneath what may appear as chaos and randomness.

If you listen carefully to the experiences shared by friends, family, and colleagues you can hear people express the same feelings about how they experienced new connections, became aware of themselves, felt more gratitude, or enjoyed the company of strangers. Love is pervading our planet. Stay tuned to it. It can relieve our stress, give us the power to find new answers to old problems and carry us well into the next phase of existence if we allow it to.

Astrologers are particularly good at sensing the cosmic rhythms that inundate the planet. They remind us to stay awake and pay attention because change is upon us. What they call the forces of the planets are, in fact, the great angelic beings, who affect the destiny of our planet and all planets. They work on an invisible, etheric plane and they control these great waves of energy coming to us now. These waves touch the lives of all living beings.

The angelic realm can help us create inner stability during these times of intense flux and change on our planet. They do this by aligning our subtle bodies with the pulse of these rhythmic waves of the universal life force. This is how we become attuned to these forces because they move through us.

If we stay conscious we can experience the joy of being in the now, and in the flow as these waves rock our planet, changing old, outdated systems and bringing new life in unexpected places.

In certain spots on the planet this is felt increasingly stronger than other places. The electro-magnetic grid within the earth is synonymous with the acupuncture points of our bodies. In these places where energy accumulates there is an extra charge. Sometimes this is experienced as very destabilizing. If a person is not familiar with subtle energies and has not developed the capacity to digest this new energy they may feel strange, or even crazy.

If we are not open in our subtle energy bodies taking in this energy and are unable to assimilate it properly we can become feverish, agitated and confused. Our "circuits" become overcharged in these environments and we may need more rest, quieter times alone, to be able to process these planetary changes. It takes discipline and groundedness to walk in everyday reality in these energy hot spots.

Angels guide us to and through these vortices of energy. At times we will be guided to these vortices to take in more energy so as to fulfill our tasks on earth. There are stories of people being transformed in the healing temples of Egypt, the sacred land of Israel, the energy vortices of Sedona and the shamanic surroundings of native people around the world. Mount Shasta, as well as some of the holy mountains of Asia, is a beacon of energy that transmits cosmic waves of energy to large areas of the planet. They have been known to bring healing and light to millions of people. Here the angelic forces are able to work directly with large groups of people who are in need of healing and transformation.

The native people of these areas are the designated keepers of sacred wisdom encoded by the great earth angels to protect and guard the land. These sites exist all over the globe. Some are better known than others, but all act as repositories of this sacred cosmic energy.

Here one can experience the Divine Presence easily because the veil is thin. In these areas truth can be easily revealed to you, and your awareness can become heightened. Here you may have a deep spiritual connection with all life, visible and invisible. If you are open to this experience it will be wonderful. If you are not prepared you may feel very disoriented and crave the security of what is known to you and familiar.

As individuals we can experience this pulse flowing through our own bodies at any time. We don't need the heightened experience of an energy vortex to intensify the energy. However, we do need a regular routine of movement and exercise because this helps distribute the energy throughout our entire body.

Daily movement routines bring the will into the body but they also open the channels to release stagnant energy so new forces can work within us. It is sufficient for most people to experience the gentle pulse in the spinal fluids that, when balanced, echo the loving rhythm of the universe.

Angels strive to create a healthy mental framework and spiritual state within us each day. We can assist them by developing a good physical routine that lets us perspire, move and stretch our muscles. They work within us every night when we sleep to help bring balance and healing to us, helping us forget the day and move into the bliss of dreamland where they bring healing to our spirits. Their medium is found in the cranial-spinal fluid that pulses through our bodies. This rhythm is called the Cranio-Sacral pulse.

When it is palpated it feels like the great infinity signs, looping into a figure eight. Coursing through the body, this pulse feeds every nerve fiber of our body. When completely balanced we experience feeling aligned and attuned to the world, and, ultimately, to all creation.

There is scientific proof of this pulse and an energetic basis for understanding how it works. Besides being deeply soothing and comforting it helps us align to the cosmic rhythms which bring healing to the body, stabilize the emotions and release the overload of accumulated mental energy we lodge every day in our body. Angels work within this fluid to move energy from the deeper centers, known as chakras, throughout our physical body.

The interesting thing about this cranio-sacral system is that it can be influenced by our thoughts. When we say to ourselves that we are balanced then the cranio-sacral system will automatically balance itself. It is responsive to affirmation. In the resonance we create with our thoughts we affect the whole universe and we affect our own cranial pulse. It is a very powerful thing to recognize that we have a force for the greater good and our personal good right at our fingertips.

What this suggests is that we can transform our lives, and the world. Our thoughts have power to influence our bodies, minds and spirits. Angels work with us to co-create our lives by inspiring us to think positive thoughts that allow the good to enter our lives. Through prayer and petition, meditation and reflective practice, we have all the tools we need to access the spiritual realm for our good and the good of the world.

Angels carry our dreams and hopes to the Source; they support our earthly desires for love, health and prosperity. They always understand, without judgment or punishment, our longings and desires as part of what we claim for our happiness and fulfillment. They know we want love and healing, and they help us realize this is possible. If we can imagine it for ourselves we can create it in our lives.

The more we purify our thinking, ridding our minds of negativity and allowing loving thoughts to flow through us, the stronger and more fully our desires will manifest in physical reality. The more we manifest our experience on the physical plane the more confident we are in the power of God and His angels to bring love and healing to us.

Transforming our thoughts truly changes our circumstances. The more we say yes to ourselves and to life the better our lives become, the more the world finds joy and peace through positive thoughts, and the more everyone thrives. We all want to experience the sweetness, joy and ease of life. When we are aligned with Source our angels can flood our consciousness with love. There is an unending supply waiting to be claimed. As we release thoughts of love out into the universe they will come back to us a thousand fold and make our world a sweeter, more joyful place in which we all can thrive and be at peace.

The Human Energy System:
The Subtle Bodies

By working within our energy field the angelic realm inspires our thinking, feeling and will. They reside in the core of the chakras which are energy power centers located within the etheric body. They address our challenges and life issues by stimulating, toning and balancing the four subtle bodies held within the human energy system.

The four bodies, which I mentioned earlier, are known as the physical body, which is our flesh and blood body; the energy, or etheric body, which is our energetic body and emotional body; the spiritual, or astral body, which is our mental body, and seat of the spirit; and the soul, or egoic body, the spirit body which contains the soul. This egoic body controls our spiritual evolution and brings us closer to realizing the truth of ourselves as aspects of God.

The angelic realm informs, inspires and instructs each of these bodies to insure healthy regulation of all cells, organs and systems. In order to create higher consciousness these four bodies work together, stay balanced and support the spirit in its growth and development. Angels are always striving to bring balance to our forces and keep harmony within this system.

The Physical Body

The physical body contains our animal vitality. It controls the precision functioning of our neuro-reflexes, and monitors motor and sensory processing. It is the most material and mineralized of the four bodies. It has no "mind" of its own, but reflects the attitudes and beliefs lodged in the higher mind.

The physical body is composed of all the elements found within the cosmos. These elements are found in traces in all organs and tissues. We are the periodic table of elements and each element has a metaphysical counterpart that supports our spiritual, as well as our physical evolution. It is said there are angels for each one of the elements.

The physical body responds directly to our thoughts and beliefs. Our thoughts are tangible entities which have the power to transform energy and influence matter. Taking responsibility for our thoughts allows us to create our reality, and transform the physical body in the process.

We can influence how we feel in our physical body by releasing the many negative thoughts which literally weigh our spirit down. These thoughts limit our experience of love and joy and stop the flow of serotonin, the "feel-good" hormone produced in the brain, when we think good thoughts.

By re-programming the mind to allow more pleasure, greater fulfillment and infinite joy into our lives we help the physical body stay strong and healthy for many years, defying aging, and counteracting any morbid attitudes where atrophy and death hold sway.

Our thoughts can make the difference between feeling good or feeling bad. If we trust in the power of the body to right itself we can become more beautiful and vital as we mature and have more resilience and stamina than we did when we were younger. We can also cure illness with this consciousness.

The physical body also is the repository for our genetic code. This defines our pre-disposition to health and disease. We have the ability, through the medium of prayer and meditation and positive affirmation, to transform our genetic material. We do this by honoring the truth of ourselves as a whole, and knowing we live in God. We allow ourselves to find peace and joy in our lives, no matter what the circumstances, and we cultivate gratitude for all we have and know. This will help the body detoxify itself of all negative content. It will open the door for healing old attitudes about insufficiency and lack that create the genetic code.

When we accept good as our natural state we transform our negative heritage into one that allows for more joy, greater fulfillment and ease, and real pleasure. In other words, life ceases to be a struggle and we can release the negative attitudes our ancestors passed down through mother's milk that said life is hard and no one wins without struggle.

It is attitudes like this, programmed into our unconscious mind, that create the living reality we believe to be true. Angels help us see that there is another way of living based on faith, trust and wholeness. Within this context life is ageless and energy flows with grace and goodness. Our bodies will reflect anything we program them to believe. Why not choose the good, and release that which makes life drudgery.

Every healthy and loving attitude about our self and life has an influence on our genetic code. A belief in good transforms our cells and fortifies us. It attunes our cellular vibration to the music of the spheres where angels dance, sing and share their love with all creation. Why not choose the good?

In truth, no one is compelled to live out an unpleasant or difficult fate, or suffer the challenges their ancestors struggled and suffered with unless they choose to do that. It heals our ancestors to release these negative thoughts from our body. It frees their spirits to go to higher planes of consciousness knowing we can be responsible for healing our lives. It allows them to reclaim the truth of who they are as spirit. It also frees the generations to come from carrying the burden of suffering they would otherwise be compelled to experience and make conscious. Clearing the genetic pre-disposition to disease frees the next generation to be more creative, more loving and the true peace makers.

The physical body is the temple for the soul. Within it lives all that we need to stay healthy and vital. Our job is to give it sufficient exercise, good nutrition, ample rest and a lot of pleasure as the necessary components that will support life in its fullest and most optimal state. Holistic medicine and a natural lifestyle also enhance well-being and make regaining balance possible.

Pain, illness and stress disturb the natural rhythms and vibrational integrity of the physical body. In order to preserve its harmony the body must have its needs met for touch, care and tenderness. The body expands in pleasure and contracts in pain.

If we want to increase our vitality and experience more energy, we are asked to open our hearts to love and think, act and be positive. This way we will give the body, as well as the spirit, what it needs. When we sacrifice the body to surgery, use harsh medications, or fall into the abuse of recreational drugs, we limit our internal capacity to connect with our spirit and live in God. Angels are challenged to reach our minds and help us evolve.

Our responsibility is to care for and nourish the physical body. It is the temple of the soul and thrives when we honor it as the Holy of Holies. The physical body incubates our soul forces throughout our life. It holds the imprint of the Divine Presence and the angelic forces working within it.

Angels help keep the physical body strong and healthy. We can learn to become our own good mother and take care of ourselves as if it was a young child that needed attention. Going without sleep, eating junk food, not exercising or stretching the body creates stagnation. It invites atrophy to set in.

The body must be fed well, hydrated sufficiently and loved for the good job it does in supporting our life. Treating it with respect is what is required of us. How we treat our body is how we treat our spirit.

The physical body is energized through the higher bodies that control feeling and thinking functions. When we create thoughts of pleasure, fulfillment and joy we give the body the possibility to expand and heal wounds of separation and pain. We let the body off the hook of having to perform like a machine. It must have sufficient rest and happy experiences to ease its way through life. This way it has the opportunity to accumulate more vital energy to do its work properly.

The physical body can endure and survive many harsh ordeals. Trauma is the single greatest obstacle to the well-being of the physical body. When nerve cells are damaged, either through accidents, surgery or accumulated stress, the physical body becomes numb and frozen. It loses its capacity to respond in a normal, healthy way to the positive and negative stimulation life holds. Without our ability to recognize and feel pain and pleasure we lose our connection to our body. We need to know when we are hungry or tired, when we feel good in our bodies or when we feel bad. How else can we make a change?

For a strong spiritual life we need a vibrant physical body that is resilient against the influx of stress. This will keep the portals of our consciousness open to the workings of the angelic realm. When we are numb or closed down the physical body will use all its energy for survival. It will deplete the higher centers in order to focus on staying alive rather than thriving. When this happens we function at minimal capacity. We lose the joy and bliss of the body. It is capable of experiencing such pleasure, which is a major component of healing.

When the body is released from trauma it has the natural capacity to sustain itself without drawing on and depleting the higher centers. It has its own optimal outlets for expression that reflect in us feeling well and loving life. The life of the body is an important aspect to maintaining higher consciousness.

We can call on our angels to bring us balance. They can help regulate our physical body and whisper in our ear when we need an adjustment in diet, rest and exercise, or require more pleasure. They can support our physical well-being in the following ways: by keeping our nervous system tranquil and focused when we are under stress; and by helping to manage all our vital systems, including regulating our heart, our blood pressure, or hormones. They can keep our bowels working and our blood purified.

The more we allow the spiritual aspect of healing to come into consciousness the less we need to rely on medical intervention to keep the physical body regulated. We have within our grasp the kindness, love and help of the spiritual world to carry us through the challenges and difficulties of life. They bring us healing at every level. Let's learn to trust it and call on it for all our needs.

Please be aware that if you have a serious physical condition you do need to see a medical doctor. What is being suggested is that you may wish to consider bringing in a spiritual component to your health and hygiene that keeps your physical body working on behalf of your deeper Self. This is the greatest power we have for our health and it is worthy of calling upon when needed.

The Angel of the Physical Body
The Angel of the Physical Body works to keep you steady, stable and healthy. It can help regulate your health and bring you the healing you need for your spirit. This allows you to fulfill your

tasks and enjoy your life more fully. This angel can support you fight against addictions and cravings which can destroy your well-being and weaken your vitality. It can also bring order to any bodily function that is out of balance by addressing the energetic and spiritual part that may be blocking your well-being.

You can ask the angel of your physical body to align you to your highest vibration so you can receive all the benefits it can offer you. More energy helps you complete your daily tasks and gives you ample vitality for fun and to enjoy your life.

You can ask this angel for high immunity to keep you strong. You can pray for a resilient healthy body that keeps you moving through life with optimal efficiency throughout your life.

MEDITATION

Sit quietly and take several deep breaths. Release any tension you experience in your body by breathing into this area. Adjust your back and neck so you feel connected and aligned to yourself. Relax your shoulders, drop your jaw, and let your eyes relax into the back of your head. Continue to breathe evenly and easily as you relax and ease down into your body.

Reflect on how you would like to feel in your body. Would you like more ease and strength, more fluidity or flexibility? Would you like to feel that your body supports you in your work, as well as in your pursuit of joy and pleasure?

Open your mind to receiving your highest guidance from the Angel of your Physical Body. Listen carefully for direct knowledge that will support your well-being. You may hear a message which could lead you to obtain a certain

for you, or a vitamin supplement which
u may have a sense that a yoga class or
support your body's efforts to achieve
tion. Listen and pay attention to your
stay open to it.

Perhaps you feel your body is tired and overworked.
It may need more rest and quiet time. When you pay
attention to your body's needs it can receive the care,
attention and help it needs. Daily meditation can include
a body scan, and a check-in to see how you feel in your
body. Take a moment to ask your angel what will support
your physical well-being.

PRAYER

Beloved Angel of my Physical Body, I call on you to
help me achieve higher levels of health, beauty and
well-being. Guide me to know what will serve me in
becoming stronger, gaining more flexibility, suppleness
and grace. Show me how I can have a stronger heart,
better functioning lungs, greater digestion and optimal
function in all my vital organs. Help me reduce those
elements in my nutrition which weaken me and make
me feel bad. Help me eliminate anything that is
harmful to my health. I pray for your guidance to keep
me strong, vital and resilient long into my old age. I
want to have all my organs, all my body parts and all
my teeth intact for years to come. Help me enjoy my
physical life fully for as long as possible.

AFFIRMATION

I affirm my right to love and enjoy my physical body till the end of my life. I listen to the wisdom of my body and do what is best for it.

THE RIGHT OF THE PHYSICAL BODY

It is my right to be healthy, active and balanced throughout my whole life.

The Etheric Body

The etheric body is the energy sheath which sits next to the physical body. It contains seven major power centers, known as chakras, which conduct the flow of life energy into the ductless glands of the body. This stimulates hormonal production. These hormones, in turn, stimulate the vital organs and bring energy and healing to the physical body.

The chakras are repositories of stamina, resilience and immunity. They also hold the energy of our beliefs and attitudes which magnetize our experiences to us. They are the medium in which healing can take place, and they are the channels through which energy moves. They are the conduits of the life force.

How Thinking Reflects In Our Experiences

If we want to understand what our beliefs and attitudes are about life we can get feedback from our experiences. If we have a joyful and positive experience we know that we have released old, negative ideas which limit our happiness. Happiness signifies that something has been resolved that may have been holding us back in the past.

When we have a less than optimal experience we learn that we must shift our thinking. We want to look at every experience, particularly the negative ones, as feedback so that there is something to learn and re-program. Both the good and the challenging experiences come from the Source. We can choose to turn any situation around which limits the truth of ourselves.

When we have a negative experience we can ask what is to be learned here. What are our attitudes regarding victimhood, martyrdom and being a servant. What stops us from fully expressing our truth and standing up for ourselves in the light of our empowerment and the truth of our healing.

We can affect our inner sense of peace and well-being through our thoughts, and we can know we are more than our experiences, which are showing us what wants to be transformed. We can always choose to change our beliefs.

How we think and what we believe impacts our well-being at every level. Our attitudes actually control the flow of energy in our bodies. They directly influence the energy flowing through the chakras. If we desire higher levels of health and well-being we must release self-limiting beliefs. They act as dampers to our well-being and vitality. We do this by choosing a higher and more vibrant thought that supports the best of us.

To God and His angels we are truly meant to know our magnificence at all levels. In order to have a healthy life we must fortify our minds with healthy attitudes. Negative thinking holds us back and, at the same time, limits the good that comes to us. If we want vitality and energy we must transform our thoughts because our entire etheric field, and our physical body, is influenced by our thinking.

Angels can help us transform our thinking to higher levels of vibration and provide a more qualitative thought process. They support and purify our energy in every way that will insure health and happiness. They work directly within our hearts and minds, through the chakra system, in all the subtle bodies, to hold an image of goodness on which we can model our thoughts.

When we are negative, and fail to affirm our worth and the goodness of life, we draw more of the same misery to us. Each time we are willing to look within and harvest out the negativity that blocks our good the more we draw that goodness into our lives. Angels work hard to stop energy leaks which weaken us and keep our vibrational field limited and low-functioning. If negativity persists it will ultimately affect our physical health.

Angels encourage us to release our fears and negative thoughts by knowing we are of value. However we do this, we begin the process of growth and healing that helps us know the truth of who we are, experience our worth, and strive to keep our energy system intact. Angels work to see we create a "realm of possibility" for our future good. They help us cultivate positive experiences that build confidence and strengthen our sense of personal identity. They want us to choose wholesome beliefs in ourselves that affirm we are worthy of love, kindness and respect.

Angels teach us to close our field down to protect us from energy leaks that diminish our strength and compromise our power. Their love for us motivates us to be strong, empowered and in the full glory of our being. Their prayer for us is that we eventually come to realize who we are and that we know we are worthy of the love we say we want. They celebrate when we stop giving our energy away to others because we don't know the truth of ourselves and have a limited sense of our value.

Angels channel only the good into us. They work with the higher energies of love, wisdom and guidance to bring us to a place of balance. How we work with the energies we experience is our free choice. They simply want us moving forward in our lives as joyfully as possible.

They impact the chakras at the most profound levels to create this balance. They see the true potential in everyone and know the magnificence of each individual so their ministering is focused on the expression of that. They know we all qualify for God's love because we are made in God and it is the greatest of God's qualities that are woven into our energy system.

Angels know we are all worthy of love and that we have nothing to prove, and no one to impress. Feeling love is the natural expression in all people. What angels can do is help remove the impediments to that outflow of love. They want us to be fully ourselves, natural in goodness, generous of spirit and willing to do and be our best. They love us just as we are and ask only that we receive the gifts they offer.

Because they are beings of pure love they are incapable of ever ceasing to love us. That would be contrary to their nature. We can experience their love during reflective moments, when we are in meditation or in extraordinary states of grace. To experience their love is confirmation that the Divine Presence is always with us, always working to bring us healing and joy, greater satisfaction and the truth of our selves at all times. This is the energy of God which is working in our energy fields.

When we feel safe, protected and loved we can easily allow more of the Presence to flow through us. We draw in more of the good when we are happy because this vibration acts as a magnet for more of itself. When we are in distress, not trusting in the goodness of life, we block that flow from entering our experience. We struggle to accomplish our tasks because our spirit is low and not able to call the good to itself for what it needs and longs for.

An important concept to register is that the angelic realm is

ALWAYS on our side. They are deeply committed to our individual happiness and well-being. They want to see us feel content and fulfilled, loved and cherished. They stand by and watch us suffer with our martyrdom and resistance to joy and they ponder why we would enjoy doing that. They only know how to relate to us through love. It is the language of our spirit. Our job is to allow their love and grace to enter our body, mind and spirit.

The Angel of the Etheric Body

The Angel of the Etheric Body resides within your energy field. It keeps you steady, balanced and aligned with your purpose. It allows vital life energy to work through your field, enter your physical body and give you ample vitality to accomplish your tasks. This angel helps you conserve energy and not become a victim of energy leaks which deplete you and weaken you.

It can help release trauma and shock which freeze the central nervous system. It can help you forget the accidents and trauma of your past so that you can thrive in the now, in joy, in happiness. This angel of your etheric body can support you in claiming your good for all that you know yourself to be. Your job is to find your value and affirm your worth. They ask that you always honor your choices for love, even if that love was not received or accepted.

The Angel of the Etheric Body resides within your field and works within each chakra to create balance, joy and harmony. It works to preserve your life force and strengthen your reserves of energy so that you have enough for times of challenge and crisis. It lets you know when you need to rest and replenish yourself, when you can be active, and when you have enough reserves to take risks and experience adventures.

This angel acts as an energy gauge for the amount of energy you have available for your life. It can help you develop reserves

23

through cultivating healthy lifestyle choices and establishing disciplined rhythms which empower your life. It can support you in creating a healthy, balanced life that is in tune with the higher harmonies of the season, and the cycles of the year.

MEDITATION

Sit quietly and take several deep breaths. Release any tension you may be feeling in your body. Pay attention to where that tension has accumulated. Perhaps you feel it in your neck and shoulders, or in your lower back.

Areas of the body that are congested and tight can indicate which chakra is being stressed. Pay attention to where your tension exists. If it is in your lower body it will most likely correspond to one of the lower centers. If it is in your upper body it will correspond to one of your higher centers.

You can tune into your body and check your energy field to see what chakras are engaged. See if the chakra and the areas of tension can give you a sense of what is blocked in you. By affirming yourself you can release this tension. Learn to use your mind to release what holds you down physically and energetically. This gives you mastery over your physical body and helps you create an energy field which is whole, clear and purified.

PRAYER

Beloved Angel of my Etheric Body, please help me organize my energy field so that I am balanced and am able to experience the wholeness of my being. I ask that any chakra that is congested or arrested releases the emotional content of past experience. I know this will let me free myself of what holds me back from being in joy and happiness. I pray that any incomplete experience where I need to forgive another be brought into my consciousness and released. Please help me to clear my field and open my heart to new possibilities for healing.

AFFIRMATION

I affirm I am a being of light, living in the present moment as a part of the divine flow that animates my spirit and fortifies my soul.

THE RIGHT OF THE ETHERIC BODY

I acknowledge the right to my own energy. I create healthy boundaries that protect and honor the truth of who I am.

The Astral Body

The astral body is the energy sheath between the etheric body and the egoic body. It contains all our thoughts, beliefs and attitudes about life. It works on our mentality to strengthen our mind and fortify our thought processes. When it is strong we have very clear thoughts and can follow them through to logical conclusions.

The astral body is the seat of the spirit, which shines whenever we affirm our self and honor our choices to love. It is the body of longing, hope and faith. It governs all our desires and aversions. Decisions about whether we like corn or broccoli get made in the astral body. Whether we vote "yea" or "nay" to something is a function of our astrality.

Our decisions and choices are based on our ideas about what is good for us and what is not. Our thinking generally holds the conventional wisdom about what our culture values and what it finds distasteful or repugnant. Developing a viable astral field helps us make choices that reach a very high level of discernment. Cultivating this body means looking carefully at what will honor the spirit.

A strong and clear astral field is always open to new ideas. It is able to adapt to change and accommodate itself to new situations, new people and new thoughts. This indicates whether a person is open to learning and is able to assimilate new ways of perceiving reality.

The astral body can become rigidified from repetition and habit, making it difficult to change and unreceptive to the new. It can hang onto ideas that it is always right, even against valuable evidence that something else may be good or equally as effective. The ability to adapt to change is a function of a fluid and flexible astral body.

The astral body is strengthened through prayer and meditation. It is purified through self-awareness and expanded through the release of self-limiting attitudes where we see ourselves as unworthy and insignificant. Where the etheric body was benefited by keeping energy flowing, the astral body is benefited by keeping our thoughts current, uncluttered and focused on the highest good.

The astral body, when toned and strong, allows us to think about our life and our situations with clarity and precision. It looks at thinking patterns that help us arrive at the best solution for us. It is seldom, in its healthy state, reactive, volatile or dulled. Keeping a strong astral field requires the ability to discern if someone or something is for our highest good and greatest joy.

The Angel of the Astral Body

The Angel of the Astral Body has the ability to release old and time-worn thoughts and cultural ideals that block our happiness and well-being. When we focus our attention on any subject it is the astral body that will receive the impressions, and conclude whether they are good for us or bad. A mature astral field is skilled at weighing the advantages and disadvantages of an action.

Through thinking and reflection about one situation or person we come to understand another. We cultivate ways of looking at life in a way that allows for optimal healing to happen. We reflect on ways that will make our lives better and more enriched. We want to build a strong astral body that allows us the benefit of our higher mind. This is always working to assist us in what we do and how we do it.

We can call on the Angel of the Astral Body to guide us through serious reflection about who we are and what our purpose is in this life. We can receive guidance about our path, our work, our health, and our relationships by keeping the space of our mind uncluttered with menial information. The mind likes to ponder on what works, what benefits, what heals and what makes for happiness. Too much electronic input keeps us from truly reflecting on what is good, spiritual, whole and worth loving.

This angel can guide us beyond the duality of the material world into the world of pure ideals, and archetypes of empowerment, responsibility and freedom. It can help us consider what our place is in the universe and where we belong in life. It can show us with whom we wish to share ourselves and how we want to be players in the game of life.

This angel can help us see the truth of ourselves as worthy of all we seek and wish to accomplish. It helps us develop loving and joyful connections with others. It can help us discern who and what we are for our highest good and greatest joy.

MEDITATION

Sit quietly and take several deep breaths. Clear your mind of the events of the day. Focus on deepening your breath and releasing any tension you have accumulated through the course of the day. Begin reflecting on a problem that you would like to have solved. This can be anything that you find you need an answer for.

As you think about this problem, pose a question in your mind such as, "How do I see my way forward in this situation?" Breathe deeply. Wait quietly as you focus your attention on this question. Allow yourself to reflect on the answer you receive. This comes from the Angel of your Astral Body and it needs you to accept its guidance and to reflect on it before you choose. You always have choice in what you want to know. Trust what you hear. If you need to ask another question prepare it and present it. It may be in regard to your first question or completely separate. Listen quietly for the answer and trust that what comes is correct.

As you think clearly about issues that require reflection you will find your mind getting sharper and you will begin to cultivate your intuition to reach higher levels of truth and knowing. This angel can give you the knowledge you require to see a bigger picture and a solution you can agree upon. You can practice this exercise for any situation or problem you face.

PRAYER

Beloved Angel of my Astral Body, help me clarify my thinking so it is crystal clear. Help me trust the truth of your guidance and know it comes from you with love for who I am. The truth of all situations and relationships is available to me when I want to know. Please be with me as I make my way in life to make good choices that serve my growth and healing. Show me how to implement the information and knowledge I receive so I may put it to good use. I am grateful for the ability to use my mind in the service of consciousness and for the greater good. Help me stay focused and intent on positive outcomes that benefit me and the community around me.

AFFIRMATION

I affirm the power of my mind to create an answer for
any problem I face. I know the higher mind comes from
God and carries all knowledge and truth within it.

THE RIGHT OF THE ASTRAL BODY

My right is to trust and cultivate my mind to serve my
God-Self to create a happy and fulfilling life.

The Egoic Body

The egoic body is the last body in our field and the furthest from
the physical body. It extends outwards from the body. It is known
as the seat of the soul. It holds the spiritual forces that determine
our destiny. It carries a myriad of life lessons from past incarna-
tions and eternal wisdom that keeps us spiritually informed.

The egoic forces create our guardian angel who protects us
and the portals to our soul. As we clear our minds of old ideas
and open up the opportunity of fulfilling our destiny, our sensitivity and refined spiritual energy need protection. They are not to
be treated in an ordinary way. They require cultivation, purifica-
tion and protection. That is what our guardian offers us.

The egoic forces relate to our sense of personal identity and
who we are at a higher level. The ego has a greater and a lesser
aspect to it that define our social personality and our spiritual
soul. At a lower level the ego learns to negotiate in the world, and
at the same time it realizes this is not enough. At a certain age it
will begin the process of aligning itself with the soul. It will want
to discover more about the way spirit leads and guides us and

what we can expect from this path of truth. It will look into religions, spiritual truths, seek guidance from within and, eventually, take responsibility for creating happiness and joy.

It takes a developed ego to open a pathway for our greater good to come to us. We want to give it recognition as a spiritual force within us and not as a lower force that keeps us from the truth of ourselves.

Our egoic body thrives when we are living a happy and joyful life, and are happily anchored in love. It rejoices when we are healthy, and have a wholesome sense of ourselves. When the ego realizes how simple life is and how easily it can flow it releases its grip on having to survive in the world and can rest in the arms of God. This gives the soul peace and tranquility in which to thrive and to ground itself in a healthy reality capable of channeling divine wisdom for itself.

Angels work with the soul forces to help formulate the experiences we need to grow, heal and realize the truth of our value. They work to open the portals for higher spiritual energy to permeate our soul so it matures and knows the wonder of life.

It is with these energies that we formulate our relationship with God as the living presence within us. We learn to accept the grace and goodness of His angels and walk the path of light, assured that all is well. It is from this energy body that we receive our highest good.

Angels nourish the soul throughout our life. They help us develop patience and faith in the goodness of the Divine. They see us safely through our challenges and initiations and, at each level of participation, they salute us for waking up to higher and higher truths. They bless us with grace and they reinforce our healing so that we are well prepared for the shocks, losses and trials that come with life.

Mostly, the angels of this body support us in realizing our innate worth and unbelievable value. They open clear channels for us to experience God's love and know His blessings. In this body we know that all good comes to us because of who we are and what we rightfully choose.

The Angel of the Egoic Body

The Angel of the Egoic Body could best be described as a guardian of our soul. This angel has passed countless lifetimes with us, guiding our soul in its growth from a young, unformed and unaware aspect of God to an awakened and enlightened soul able to be responsible for its choices and eager to create peace, happiness and joy for itself. By doing this the world becomes a far better place for all to live within the presence of love.

We commune with this angel through prayer and meditation, asking it to awaken our consciousness so we can experience the truth of our being. We ask to be capable, responsible and joyful as we share the best of ourselves. This angel supports our soul's participation in creative, joyful and pleasurable ways that are safe, fun and healthy. It honors our needs for individual self-expression, and wholesome inquiry into the truths of life. This angel supports our living fully in the best ways that give us joy and peace.

We can call on this angel for help to move us past barriers of fantasy into realms of understanding and gratitude. Without gratitude this angel would not be able to hear our requests. At the egoic level we have forgiven the past, blessed the present and opened our hearts to the future with gratitude for how it is.

MEDITATION

Sit quietly and take several deep breaths. Breathe into any area of tension you may be holding on to. Release this tension with your breath. As you sit quietly, reflect on your life's path. Think of the difficult and challenging times you have suffered and the great joys of your life as well. Give thanks for all these moments as you realize their importance in your life. Forgive those that have hurt you, move forward in joy and open a channel for your good to come to you. There may be challenging people you engaged with, or unwholesome events you experienced, but they are in the past. Find your gratitude for the present and be willing to create more joy, more ease, more pleasure for yourself. Everything you have done has created core strength and power for you.

We have so much to be grateful for in life. There are experiences that may have tested us beyond our limit. They surely extended our capacity to cope. These are the defining experiences that build inner strength. Celebrate your capacity to experience them, acknowledge yourself and think of happy and joyful things you would like to do that will make you feel you deserve pleasure and peace. Again, be grateful for the challenges of those hard times. It is through those moments that we are who we are today and better able to appreciate the joy of now.

PRAYER

Beloved Angel of my Egoic Body, thank you for
the experiences that have molded and defined me.
I know you are always with me, helping me through
each challenge with your light and grace. I know
I am not always receptive to receiving my good and
I do apologize for that. I want to express my deep
and humble gratitude for all the difficult people I
have encountered, all the menacing and threatening
situations that caused me to turn inward and trust
in God. I appreciate all the times I thought I would
fail and be lost. Thank you for carrying me through
each situation, each encounter and keeping me
steady, time and time again. I am so grateful.

AFFIRMATION

I affirm the strength of God working in me in every
challenge of my life. I know everything is for my good.
I rejoice and celebrate my life.

THE RIGHT OF THE EGOIC BODY

I claim my right to know the truth of me and that
I am always held in love by the forces of God
and His angels.

CHAPTER 2

The Chakras and the Angelic Realm

Understanding Chakras and How They Work

Chakras are energy power centers that reside within the etheric body, which is the subtle body next to our physical body. Chakra is a word from Sanskrit, the sacred language of the Hindus. It means "wheel of light." It refers to the whirling, spinning action of these non-anatomical centers where energy flows and is conducted into the physical body. Chakras are the link between the energy flow found in the etheric body and the hormone-secreting ductless glands found in the physical body.

Here is a simple explanation of how this energy works. Energy moves through the physical body from the core of the earth and from the far reaches of the cosmos. These are the two primal sources of life energy found in all planetary life. They represent the electro-magnetic streams that sustain life on earth. Chakras are the conduits of these two poles of energy. They sustain the life of the physical body.

Within the etheric body there exist seven major chakra centers and 21 minor chakras. All the acupuncture points are also chakras. The etheric body acts as a hydraulic pump which moves energy into and out of the chakras. The chakras supply the energy or fuel to the physical body and provide vital energy to the physical centers. It does this by stimulating the ductless glands to produce and supply hormones. The various hormones affect all vital organ activity in the human body.

The hormones connected with the chakras are:

- the adrenocorticol and adrenomedullary hormones produced by the adrenal cortex of the kidneys, which are connected to the Root Chakra;
- female and male hormones found in the ovaries of women and testes in men such as estrogenic and androgenic hormones and follicle-stimulating hormones, which are connected to the Sacral Chakra;
- pancreatin, gastrin and intestinal hormones secreted by the pancreas, which is related to the Solar Plexus Chakra;
- thymus gland hormones that support immunity early in life which are produced by the thymus gland and relate to the Heart Chakra;
- thyroid and thyrotropic hormones secreted by the thyroid gland, which is connected to the Throat Chakra;
- pituitary-secreting hormones that are connected with growth, and secondary sexual characteristics, secreted by the lobes of the pituitary gland, which are associated with the Brow Chakra;
- melatonin and cyclical-stimulating hormones secreted by the pineal gland, which are related to the Crown Chakra.

The chakras are placed near these ductless glands along the spine. They start at the base of the spine with the Root Chakra and move upward, distributing energy along the spinal nerve ganglions, till they reach the crown of the head.

Their size is dependent on age. They can be as small as a few centimeters in circumference at birth and grow into large, expansive wheels of light that cover the entire body and radiate several feet from the body's center.

This expansion happens as we mature and develop. As we become conscious, grow mentally, emotionally and spiritually, these centers blossom and expand outward. The chakras are the energetic expression of our vitality, awareness and emotions.

The Vital Force

The vital force that courses through the chakras governs physical growth in children and young adults and mental and emotional development in adults. It helps each chakra expand to meet the needs and requirements of its particular function.

Eventually the vital force will stop focusing on physical growth and work within the higher mental centers to foster maturity and appropriate adult responses to life, such as the ability to relate, bond and connect with others and choose a responsible way of living and working.

The vital force, in adults, expresses itself as emotional growth, sensitivity, greater mental focus and concentration and, hopefully, the ability to abstract concepts and thoughts. It will become highly refined by the time we pass 40 years old and transform itself into spiritual energy and conscious awareness.

For instance, the Root Chakra conducts life energy into the

survival and growth of a child up until age seven. From that age on the Sacral Chakra begins to dominate the field. This chakra governs physical growth and immunity. This is the age at which children are usually the most healthy. This chakra expands and develops until the age of fourteen when the Solar Plexus begins to take over further development.

This chakra works on forming a healthy ego development. It helps create a sense of personal identity within the young adult which is necessary for its survival in the world. This will expand and develop until age 21. This development continues through our chakras till it has reached age 49. This is when the chakras are fully developed and our spiritual development starts to take over during our senior years.

The chakras begin as a physical, life-determining activity and move from the physical plane to the emotional plane, then on to the mental plane and then the spiritual plane. At each stage of development we strive to cultivate a healthy trust in life that facilitates ease, awareness, and joy. We enjoy each phase of life development and keep this vital force moving through us in an organized, systematic way that honors life.

During the early years our talents and gifts will emerge and we begin to develop a plan for actualizing them. This will determine the path our life will take. If we are led to fulfill other people's ideas of what they think is good for us we may miss the experience of choosing a life path well suited to our gifts. A strong ego development lets us have the inner force to choose our path.

When there is arrestment or shock in a person's development the chakra will "freeze." This may be the result of illness, loss or changes that are contrary to our well-being. When someone dies who we loved, or parents divorce, or families move from familiar ground, or when there is financial reversal, our vital force becomes fixed in survival mode. We are then stuck in that energy and also in the age-appropriate chakra, till we resolve the issues and regain our vitality.

We may look back on our life to see what those events and circumstances were that altered our perception of life being safe, joyful and easy. If we connect our age at the time of the events with the corresponding chakra we will see what issues need addressing.

We can open up this field through therapy, healing or anything that lets us release the energy that was congested at the time of arrestment. Whatever we do to heal this will bring us into current time. This is how healing happens at an energetic state of development.

The chakras develop as a result of healthy attitudes and wholesome beliefs. They respond to meditation, prayer, positive affirmations, and a wholesome lifestyle. When hormonal imbalance occurs it signifies that at some level we are engaged in negative thinking or are experiencing a return to old, antiquated survival attitudes. This upsets the flow of energy in the chakras and can create, if not soon rectified, physical pathology.

It is always worthwhile examining our attitudes about life to see what beliefs are blocking our energy. If we are negative, blaming or angry then we are stuck somewhere in the past and our energy is congested. We may want to ask ourselves what the truth is for us about a particular experience or simply forgive and heal the past. Our chakras are so responsive to thought that simply thinking a positive affirmation about the past can transform their field and release old, blocked energy.

When we are living a healthy, regulated and balanced life we are able to store reserves of energy for times of duress and stress. Building these reserves keeps the body strong and makes it easy to cope with change because we draw on our blue-chip reserves to help us through challenges.

When we live in chaos and turmoil, or when the body is chronically taxed with stress, we deplete our reserves quickly. This is when we can become drained and ill. The chakras shrink and wither from too much outgoing energy and weaken our system.

It is essential to grasp that our immune system functions because of the vital flow of energy conducted through the chakras. We need to fortify our energy body from time to time with loving deeds and experiences of pleasure and fun. These are the times that sustain and nurture our being. They are good for our soul and bring us joy.

This helps transform our chakras and releases stagnation and congestion. Humor is one of the best medicines for the soul as it clears out so much negativity. The chakras are able to re-animate the entire energy body from time to time through humor.

How the Angels Work in the Chakras

Angels and the Root Chakra

The angelic realm works within the chakra centers. They work in the Root Chakra, for instance, as guardians for small babies. They support and nourish new life and help the baby to survive. They will remain focused in that chakra for the first seven years of the child's life. They are always around the child, creating strength, providing safety, and creating a healthy foundation for the child to meet new challenges.

Angelic beings create a core consciousness in each person to help serve future needs. They connect with the life force running deep within the physical body to serve the child throughout its development. They also guide the spirit, from its home in the heavens, to incarnate within the Root Chakra during the first seven years of life. This anchors the life force in the body and insures the child's growth, independence and health.

They control the formative forces flowing into the child's being and direct them towards physical growth and development. They nurture the lives of children by keeping them safe and healthy. Sometimes the child will sense these angels working within them and know them as their imaginary friends.

The Root Chakra is governed by the powerful Archangel Michael and his angels. He rules over the angelic forces that influence conception, pregnancy, childbirth, infancy and early childhood up to age seven. Michael creates stability within the Root Chakra during these early years. He develops links between the mother and baby which insure inner stability, and, ultimately, a healthy and sound baby. His energy helps form the strong bones that make up the skeletal system which will support the child and give him structure.

Angels and the Sacral Chakra

The Sacral Chakra is the next chakra up from the Root Chakra. It governs the hormonal development that leads to puberty. It influences the transformation from childhood to young adulthood. This chakra develops between ages seven and fourteen. It is located in the navel area and supplies the entire pelvic basin with energy. This is the center for sexual and procreative activity, abundance, immunity, pleasure and self-love.

The attitudes that form in this chakra need to be supportive to appropriate sexual behavior and have a healthy recognition of

41

psychological boundaries. This is when a child first walks into the adult world and it takes the child into the throes of adolescence. This can be a challenging initiation into another world for a child and it needs to be done consciously and carefully.

During this time the angelic forces keep the child safe as it explores the natural world and feels the changes happening within its own body. The angelic forces support healthy imagination and creativity, and give the child as much joy as possible during this time of its life.

The Archangel Metatron, who rules the Sacral Chakra, and the angels of this center all strive to bring balance and promote health in the child. They encourage us to enjoy ourselves, and partake in simple, playful pleasures before the responsibilities of adulthood fall on our shoulders.

Metatron and the Sacral Chakra angels provide us with a sense of ease and well-being in these young years and encourage us to play and have fun. They seek to instill a wholesome sense of balance and the right measure in all things. They set the foundation for understanding discipline, hard work and the nature of reward. They also instill a sense of rhythm that brings balance between activity and rest, appetite and exercise. They teach moderation in all things.

Angels and the Solar Plexus Chakra

The Solar Plexus Chakra controls growth from age 14 to 21. It interfaces physical growth with mental development and works to define a healthy ego and sense of personal identity. It is ruled by the Archangel Uriel and the forces of the Archai, or angel princes. This chakra is located over the area of the stomach. This chakra helps form a stable and healthy ego.

The qualities of the Solar Plexus are: self-worth, self-respect, self-esteem, confidence, personal power and freedom of choice. These qualities form the core of our ego. They are the qualities which will give a young person confidence in pursuing a good path in life. This chakra will affect a person's ability for intelligent choices throughout its life.

The Archai help instill personal confidence and foster a good sense of value and worth in a person. The age of this chakra's development corresponds to the time in early adulthood when we experiment with our image. This is when we begin to have a sense of who we are.

The physical body has reached maximum physical growth and no longer needs the energy of the vital force. This is when it can focus on developing the mental capacities of the individual to abstract concepts and define values. This is when we reach our majority and enter the world of adults so we want to be able to think intelligently about our life.

The Archangel Uriel and the Archai teach us to honor ourselves through this chakra. They work to see us develop self-respect and trust in our value. They want us to find fulfillment and happiness. They know we are truly worthy of the good we seek but sometimes we don't know that about ourselves and our ego is too weak to dream big or realize more imposing tasks.

The Archai and Archangel Uriel support our efforts at becoming young adults. They encourage us to become independent adults, with a rich sense of enthusiasm and a healthy love of adventure for life.

Angels and the Heart Chakra

The Heart Chakra governs our capacity to give and receive love. Its forces are so powerful it is regulated by three angelic beings. The heart is the center of the physical body and love is the center of the emotional body. It is love that makes life meaningful and gives us a sense of hope, purpose and joy. We seek it out and want it to find us at every opportunity. We can lose our sense of self all too easily in the hope of being loved. This is delicate territory for the angels and, at the same time, the area of life they know perfectly well. Love is, after all, what they live, breathe and know through and through.

The Heart Chakra is ruled by the Archangel Raphael and the angelic forces known as the Virtues, Dominions and Dynamis. The chakra is located in the middle of the chest over the heart. It opens between ages 21 and 28. Its focus is on love, healthy relationships, peace, joy and gratitude.

At this stage of personal development most people are ready to form emotional attachments and engage in loving relationships. This is when the heart is capable of sharing itself, and when people are able to give and receive love and experience intimacy. It is an ideal time to form deep connections that give us an opportunity to experience love.

The three angelic forces governing the Heart Chakra work to keep the heart happy, receptive and open to love. They encourage us to trust in life and find people who we can enjoy being with and share our selves with. They want us to find people who will honor and respect us, who can love us and want the best for us in life. They want us to have the courage to take a chance on love.

These three angelic forces work to strengthen the heart, both physically and emotionally. They know a broken heart can create an emotional paralysis that may interfere with other relationships formed later in life. They caution young people to have fun, take it lightly, and not rush into marriage or commitment too quickly. They want people to be sure they have the capacity to stay in a relationship through the thick and thin of life's turnings.

They encourage, guide and protect our hearts as much as possible. They know, where love is concerned, that young people do not necessarily pay close attention to their wisdom, nor do they always follow what is in their best interests. This is when angels work to repair, mend and heal broken hearts.

They know that we will eventually find our way to love again, and they see us through the heartbreak of loss and the pain of rejection. We are so blessed for their care and the love they offer us. This is such a tender time for most people and it is not easy to negotiate a loving relationship and find certainty that this person we now love will be right for us in several years' time.

The heart wants to love. That is its primary function. When it is stopped in the process of loving an individual it may expand its field to include humanity, or a group such as small children, the elderly or the handicapped. When this happens the personal heart is being repaired by the angelic forces until we are strong enough in our individuality to love again.

When the heart is ready it will love again. It may be more cautious in getting entrapped and it may be much wiser in who it chooses to be the recipient of its grace. It will, however, venture out again to find that perfect mirror of its love, in hopes that, this time, its love will be gratefully received and appreciated.

Angels and the Throat Chakra

The Throat Chakra controls our personal expression, willpower, communication and creativity. It is the center for truth and integrity. It is ruled by the Archangel Gabriel, who brings us the Word of God, and by the Seraphim. It is located in the throat and controls the mouth, teeth, ears and back of the neck. It opens between ages 28 and 36.

The Seraphim encourage us to be creative and self-expressive in our actions and in relationships. They want us speaking our truth and standing up for what we believe to be right. They know the power of the word to instill integrity, will, communication and creativity.

They work with us to express ourselves through the power of speech and truth. It is up to us to overcome our belief that no one wants to hear what we say, or that what we say is not smart enough or good enough. Thoughts and beliefs like this have kept the throat blocked and shut down for far too long.

It may take overcoming shyness and timidity to express ourselves but this is what is asked as this center for creative communication opens and grows.

Energy may be fluid and flowing all through the chakras till it reaches the Throat Chakra. Then it becomes swallowed, suppressed and controlled so that hardly a peep is heard of emotional truth and mental clarity. If a person is forced to be compliant there will be little real sharing of thoughts, ideas or dreams.

At this age many people question convention. They want a greater say in their relationships, their work and within their communities. They start to speak out. They begin to seek higher levels of empowerment and so they start to express themselves more fully.

The Seraphim can strengthen the Throat Chakra and help us commit to expressing our truth. The Throat Chakra can also link our speech to our heart so that what we say comes from the depth of our being. We want to be able to express ourselves in all manner of ways that reflect our beauty, our truth and our intellect.

Angels and the Brow Chakra

The Brow Chakra regulates and controls many bodily functions, but it is particularly developed for us to use our mental faculties for a happy and healthy life of choice and responsibility. It is the center of wisdom, knowledge, discernment, intuition and imagination.

It is governed by the Goddess Isis–Sophia, known as the Shekinah or feminine face of God, and ruled by the Cherubim. It is located between the eyebrows. It opens between ages 36 and 42. It controls our ability to synthesize thinking and vision, our inner skills like intuition and imagination, and our ability to make wise decisions about our physical life.

This is the chakra where thinking becomes joined with spirituality. It opens at the time in life when people sense their destiny unfolding. They may have a clear view of their place in the world and what they would like to do for themselves and for the world.

This is a time when they may change jobs, move house, divorce or marry, become ill, or retrain in search of their path. Change fuels this chakra's awakening.

The focus of this chakra is on cultivating a reliant inner guidance and developing strong intuitional skills which can serve to guide us on our spiritual path in life. This chakra anchors people in the highest truth of who they are. Wherever they were living before this chakra awakened may not hold the degree of satisfaction they expected. This can be the impetus for change to happen.

This can lead to avenues of self-inquiry that involve spiritual dimensions. It can bring a person to new and deeper truths about themselves and what they want for the rest of their lives. This is a time to connect to the Source within oneself.

The angelic forces of the Cherubim support these changes. They want people to realize their worth and make choices that are resonant with their higher consciousness. It may be a time to explore alternative healing, read spiritual books, visit an ashram, or meet people who walk the path of light.

All this is designed to bring about transformation and healing. It is often described as a time of renewal and revelation. The Cherubim walk with us during this time of change.

Angels and the Crown Chakra

The Crown Chakra governs serenity, beauty and our indelible connection with Source. It is governed by the Christ Light, and graced by the Holy Spirit. It is ruled over by the Thrones, the angelic beings who rest at the foot of the throne of God.

This chakra opens between ages 42 and 49. It is the center for spiritual awareness and insights. When it opens we know the truth of ourselves at a more real level then ever before. We explore spiritual dimensions, from angels to energy healing, and we know that these are realities that have credence and merit, regardless of what conventional thinking says.

This is the time in life when this chakra expresses its fullness, to re-evaluate the truths we have held to see what holds up and what does not. It is a time of examination. People often ask the question about efficacy. They want to know if their relationship can move into spiritual dimensions or if their job really is the best place for them to be.

Change is not as dramatic as it was in the last chakra but it is deeper and the questions that get asked are more profound. They will lay the spiritual foundations for the remainder of one's life.

This is a time when people seek tranquility, peace, ease and a time for inner reflection and to garner insight from their experiences.

The Thrones help us become spiritually mature. They teach us the eternal nature of spirit and the universal truths that govern all life. They help us express the power of spirit in our work, health, and relationships. They bring the grace of the Holy Spirit into our lives.

The highest spiritual forces after the angelic beings are the Holy Spirit, the Christ Light and the Divine Presence of God. We are so close to them in this center. We can work with all the spiritual forces for our healing and wholeness and recognize they are us. They exist within us as archetypal forces that affect every aspect of life. They are there to lift us up. They want to see us develop into true beings capable of giving and receiving love and bringing healing to planet earth.

What is the Aura?

What we call the aura is the fullness of the chakras expanding out into the world. It is very susceptible to our thoughts, beliefs and attitudes. It responds easily to new thoughts that are rich in love, self-acceptance and truth. It expands in love and contracts in pain and negativity.

We have the ability to heal any leaks in the aura with positive intentions, clear thoughts of love and acceptance. Many healers today work within the context of balancing and healing the chakric system. They address the energy of the auric field by channeling cosmic energy and healing affirmations into it.

We call its range the "field" because it describes the range of energy that extends out from our center. As we become more loving and connect to the higher spiritual truths that will guide our lives, the more the field expands.

When we are emotionally mature and spiritually whole we are in the flow of life. Our field is filled with the radiant energy of harmony and joy. It shines with a very beautiful pearly-white light. This can be seen by the naked eye as a light field that surrounds the body.

In the medieval and Renaissance paintings of the Christ and the Apostles, the Blessed Virgin Mary and the saints, the aura is depicted as a halo of light above their heads. This is described as the grace of the Holy Spirit descending upon them. In fact, it is their own consciousness radiating light from within them out into the world around them. They have been graced from within.

This light exists in all life forms, such as around trees, flowers, rocks and crystals. It has its greatest expression in animal life and, especially, in humans. For instance, we know that when people glow with this radiant life force their light is shining brightly. They entice us with this glow and we are, inexplicably, drawn to them.

We experience this energy as grace. It is whole, healing and supportive to all life. It sustains us, nourishes us and keeps us steady through the various turns, and highs and lows of life. It helps us move through trials and initiations that are difficult and challenging.

When we are blessed to know people whose light fills our lives we feel our own light turn on and twinkle. Once we have chosen to expand our field we release old, stagnant, tired and bitter energy. We transform the process of aging and become beautiful, no matter what our chronological age is. We regain our stamina, take better care of ourselves and move in the world in joy and happiness. This is the light of God which is living, breathing and moving in us.

We can readily experience this field in others. When we meet someone who has a presence about them we feel their vitality and we sense their warmth. When we hear an inspiring speaker we feel their aura and the brilliance of their ideas working in us. Their consciousness has touched ours. When people are in their truth their light shines and their field is visible.

We may experience this as warmth or we may feel attracted to someone without actually having any reason for it. We just like their energy field. We may experience feeling comforted in someone's presence and drawn to them without having any real knowledge of who they are or what they do. This warmth signifies a radiant field. It carries the energy of angels radiating love.

These people have often done the inner work of cleansing their belief systems and harvesting out their negative attitudes. They know who they are and they attract us because their field is radiant with love, joy and harmony. Many of the people we meet with strong auric fields live simple, healthy lives, in harmony with themselves, and are congruent with their greater good. They are happy, fulfilled, and at ease with life. No matter what their external circumstances are like they radiate well-being. They are always surrounded by hosts of angels.

Understanding the Chakras

Understanding the chakras can inform your higher mind about the depths of your inner nature. They serve as a gauge for our health, our psychology and our spiritual development. As we learn how to balance and heal the chakras we become more resonant with life, more accepting and more able to draw to us the positive experiences which will nourish and feed our spirit.

Accepting that we are more than a physical body is the first step to understanding the nature of energy healing and the power of angels. It is through the energy body that all healing happens. It is where angels reside.

It is essential to remember that all chakras contain the specific life issues and emotional challenges we need to deal with in order to evolve. Each chakra includes a particular rite of passage leading to greater freedom and spiritual awareness.

These 'rites', or rights, as we work up through the chakra system, are: the right to our life, found in the Root Chakra; the right to health, sexuality, pleasure, unconditional love, and prosperity, found in the Sacral Chakra; the right to self-worth, self-respect, self-esteem, self-confidence, personal power and freedom, found in the Solar Plexus Chakra; the right to love, peace and joy, found in the Heart Chakra; the right to truth, willpower, communication, creativity and integrity found in the Throat Chakra; the right to mental clarity, wisdom, discernment and knowledge, intuition and imagination, found in the Brow Chakra; and the right to serenity, beauty and spirituality found in the Crown Chakra.

Healing and Growth

As we integrate these archetypically inspired qualities and enjoy the rights of each chakra more fully, we expand our consciousness and develop a richer and deeper connection to the living presence within us. What we call God is the highest principal of universal love, truth and beauty that exists. Our radiance is God's grace expressing through us, as us, in us. This is what makes our field expand with light. Knowing the truth of us is what spiritual development is.

Angels are those agents of good working in us to bring about the harmony, balance and healing we need. The angelic beings regulate our function and support our structure. When we are ill, in pain, or suffering an acute condition, this is a clear indication that change is happening. This is a time to be aware of what is working in us, mentally, emotionally and morally. Consciousness can save us suffering and facilitate quick and effective healing.

Angelic beings work within an archetypal grid of higher principals which help us express our full potential for beauty, goodness and love. These are all the highest qualities of God which can be developed in humanity. These gifts are unequivocally given to each human being, despite racial, cultural or social circumstances. How they manifest is dependent on the choices we make for self-love and wholeness.

We will share these qualities with everyone we meet and they reflect our level of self-acceptance, ease, and joy that we bring to life. We will touch many lives with this light and radiance. These qualities will, ultimately, define our character and heal our spirit.

Healing is the expression of wholeness and joy we have working in us. It fulfills itself as a greater capacity to love and enjoy life. Nothing can block healing from reaching us other than our own self-imposed and self-limiting ideas of who we think we are and what we deserve. If we believe we deserve goodness and love, healing will fill our lives and we will experience true abundance. Our thoughts are ours and we can choose to see ourselves as deserving of the good.

Negative ideas are what we aim to release, at all levels of our being, because they don't serve our pursuit of happiness. They impede our growth and development and, worst of all, they keep us in an archetypal gridlock of victimhood.

Victimhood can be described as the negative state where we

blame others, blame the world, and blame God for the events and circumstances of our life. Our faith in who we are, as children of God, has the power to create happiness and joy as well as pain and suffering. We have the choice to accept and love ourselves just as we are, or we can blame and point our finger at others, blaming them for our problems and making them the cause of our suffering.

Knowing this can help you transform your life and draw the very best to yourself out of love for yourself. There is no need to be a victim because it diminishes you to a level where you abnegate responsibility for your own choices and actions. Angels will cheer you on for every life-affirming thought you have about yourself that releases this victim archetype from your consciousness.

In opening ourselves to our highest good we become connected with the great universal forces that pulse through the cosmos and bombard our planet. If we are open to receiving our good then we align our spirit with the heart of creation we know as God. We feel this energy and we direct it to places and people who need healing. We can do this simply with our thoughts. Angels will carry it to where it needs to go.

As we experience our wholeness we know all good comes to us because of who we are. We know we are worthy of what we claim for ourselves. Our lives will always follow the form our mind creates about our good. As we accept and love ourselves more fully we will enjoy greater expressions of that good manifesting in our life. It will show up as happiness, love, creativity, health, prosperity and fun. This is what heals our planet and all who live on it.

Angels will always strive to see us through the challenges and initiations we face that bring us our empowerment and lead us to the truth of who we are. They will always bring us comfort when we hurt and give us succor when we are wounded. These are part of the inevitable consequences of being human and engaging in life. We can count on that.

How we handle these events is what defines us. Angels can support us in growing into the fullness of our being, accepting our humanity and imperfections. They can help us know the deeper truth of who we are as divine expressions of God.

They know how important it is for us to grow up and take responsibility for the quality of life we want for ourselves and for our planet. Their job is not to babysit us as wounded spirits but to see us empowered as fully realized spiritual forces that can and do make a difference in the world around us. They want us to have a voice to express our heartfelt ideas and longings. They strive to open the doors of our soul to love, pleasure and joy and the wonder we call life. And they are always willing to support us in this process in any way they feel will help us.

CHAPTER 3

The Three Levels
of Heaven

Just as angels have their unique identities, so do the stages of
heaven in which they reside. Heaven is divided into three
tiers and within each tier there are three categories of angels.
The distinction between them comes from what each group of
angels does with mankind and how they act as agents of God's
love to all creatures. They all carry the light, truth and grace of
God to humanity, but in distinct and different ways.

So, there are nine categories of angels residing within these
three levels of heaven. Each level strives to transform and heal
aspects of human consciousness in a particular way. Each works
with a facet of our inner development and is suited to our levels
of understanding, spiritual awareness and inner development.

The three levels of heaven are called the Heaven of Form,
the Heaven of Creation, and the Heaven of Paradise. Within the
first level are the Angels, Archangels and Archai. Within the
second level are the Virtues, Dominions and Dynamis. Within
the third level are the Seraphim, Cherubim and Thrones. The
highest level of heaven also holds the Holy Spirit, the Blessed
Mother of God, and the Christ Light – God lives within all three
levels.

The Heaven of Form

The Heaven of Form contains the Angels, Archangels and Archai. In the human energy system the angelic beings reside within the Root Chakra, Sacral Chakra and Solar Plexus Chakra. These correspond to the Heaven of Form because they are concerned with our relation to the material, familial and tribal world. These are the chakras that hold the collective ideas of humanity.

These first three chakras, and the first level of heaven, deal with our essential beginnings, and the attitudes we developed around how we will survive in life, how we hope to experience joy and pleasure, and how we find empowerment and freedom in the choices we make regarding jobs, relationships and health.

Angels and the Root Chakra

The angels belong in the first category of heaven which we call the Heaven of Form. It is the closest level to the human plane and is easily accessible to all. Here angels offer guidance, give protection and provide for our well-being and safety. The angels bring humanity God's unconditional love for all His creatures.

They nourish us with their abiding love when we are wounded, uncertain or lost. They encourage us to find our way forward in life and they bring us overall support for our free choices. They work in the Root Chakra to ground our spirit in our physical bodies. They will stay anchored in the Root Chakra our whole life, but their primary work is done before we complete our seventh year.

This is the age when the spirit is fully incarnated within the physical body. This means the child is ready to take on individual responsibilities and is ready to have a degree of separation from the mother.

Previously, the child was enmeshed strongly with the mother's energies and lived fully within her aura. Now, at seven, the child takes on a new focus and begins to discover the world around it. It starts developing ideas and attitudes of its own regarding how it wants to play in life. The child will develop new interests of its own and be more externally focused outward towards the world, ready to explore.

Angels always stay close to children to protect and guide them. They are always creating a shield between the child and the world. They protect it from too much exposure. They mute their senses and dull their affect so they are not readily affected by conflict, struggle or unhappiness. They encourage children to explore their world within boundaries that keep them safe. Allowing children to stay young and unaware encourages the angels and gives them support for working within each child's field for a longer period of time.

This is a great gift the angels bring to children and the longer they can have that interface with angels the kinder, gentler and happier they will be as young adults. Angels help to keep children's spirits young, flexible and happy for as long as possible.

The world may encroach, from time to time, on the feelings of a child but, generally, they are immune from and do not get involved in the worries of adults. This is because angels are always diverting their focus to more amusing and interesting possibilities. All this builds a strong and resilient Root Chakra.

Archangels and the Sacral Chakra

The archangels, also part of the Heaven of Form, work within the Sacral Chakra. They are related to the qualities of light that permeate our being. They help the spirit shine brightly and they help release the impediments that limit our spirit. They support us living a wholesome, healthy lifestyle, full of pleasure, ease, and abundant good health. They calibrate the resonance of our life energy to the universal rhythms in each chakra.

The archangels define our capacity for joy and pleasure, and develop our capacity for happiness; in part through the Heaven of Form and the archangels, and also through the energy of the Sacral Chakra.

Archangels also help heal wounds that have been perpetrated against this chakra. This is very prevalent in western society. They offer healing for sexual abuse and dysfunction. They also help us balance the need for money with the need for pleasure, fun and ease. They remind us that whatever our external circumstances may be, we are always worthy of absolute unconditional love for ourselves.

When this chakra has been released of its negative load we can enjoy ourselves fully without the stricture of guilt and shame. All the angelic beings of the Heaven of Form release these negative qualities. Until this has been achieved it becomes difficult to move to higher levels of advancement in the angelic realm.

If we can manage to find the balance between hard work and play, giving and taking, as responsible adults who still value the qualities of childhood, we will heal this chakra and release ourselves from the weight of negativity. We must choose how we will find our delight and pleasures and what is fun for us.

Archangels help us define what is morally correct. They work within conventional thinking to transform ideas about suppressed sexuality, particularly in women. They strive to erase the double standard, sexual-preference bigotry and all forms of injustice and inequality related to gender and sex. They work very hard in this age to help people feel safe, loved and cherished as they mature and to help them find pleasure.

Within the Heaven of Form sexuality is valued as a form of pleasure in which people can grow and heal. When it is denied then it creates a hunger and can turn into a perversity which is not healthy or wholesome for the individual. When guilt and shame have been released the archangels of the Heaven of Form move the spirit up to the higher levels of love and awareness found in the two higher levels of heaven.

The Archai and the Solar Plexus

The Archai are the angelic beings who rule the Solar Plexus Chakra. They work to help us develop our personality, or ego. They want us to be able to encounter the forces of the world with resilience and intelligence. They build internal forces within us that allow us to meet the demands of the world and negotiate with it.

The Archai encourage us to stand up for ourselves and express our truths. They teach us, by the examples found in literature, history and modern-day entertainment, to live in truth and abide within high ethical and moral principles. They encourage us to grasp the nature of our value and build self-respect into our character.

Their work is to let us know who we are as individuals and, also, as aspects of God. They stress our oneness with all life and, at the same time, our individual nature as unique individuals. We can live within this earthly and heavenly reality by understanding that we have value. We choose our earthly encounters based on what and who is good for us and we always maintain our pride and dignity throughout.

The Archai help create a personality within us that is both independent and life-affirming. They want us to grasp our worth and know that who we are is important to us. They do not want to see us diminished, cut down or abused because we are unsure of ourselves.

They help us develop confidence in ourselves and personal power to withstand both temptations and people who seek to manipulate us with flattery, or the promise of acceptance. The age frame in which they are the most powerful is between 14 and 21, that age when people are so susceptible to external influence.

The angelic beings of the Heaven of Form work in our formative years to bring us to the threshold of adulthood with our spirit intact. They want us free of guilt and shame, proud of who we are and able to deal with the world in the best way we can. They inspire confidence, humor, inner strength and freedom of choice.

As each new generation of humanity comes forward these qualities are more firmly in place in their field. They are better able to face the world with assurance, knowing what they can do to help make it a better, safer and more peaceful place. The angels are surely doing their work within the Heaven of Form for the young people of today.

MEDITATION ON THE HEAVEN OF FORM

Sit quietly and reflect on these first three chakras that correspond to the Heaven of Form. Scan your body for tension and breathe deeply into those areas to release tension.

We all have degrees of shame and guilt that can be released. If anyone did have a perfect childhood, without the infringement of the world coming too close, they are deeply blessed. In our modern world many people face their own issues around their body and sexuality, and the shame and guilt that instills.

Forgiveness goes a long way to releasing these negative qualities. Take a deep inspiration into your lungs. Forgive yourself for anything you have done as a young person to carry shame. When you are willing to forgive yourself for your "sins" you will be free to enjoy your life now with greater degrees of pleasure and delight.

If you truly feel you did something wrong, find the compassion within your heart to release your sense of diminishment. Allow the angelic forces of the Heaven of Form to help you release all the negative beliefs about being "good enough" to be dissolved in the blessings of their love.

PRAYER

Beloved angelic forces of the Heaven of Form, thank you for your guidance, protection and love in my youth. I know I sometimes did things that were not intelligent, nor kind or self-loving. I have learned through these years that I am not bad, nor was I wrong. I ask you to help me forgive myself. I know God has already forgiven me. I wish to lay my guilt and shame aside and find true self-acceptance and deep abiding love for who I am.

AFFIRMATION

I release all negative thoughts about my self as a child.
I know I am forgiven, released and open to love and
acceptance now.

THE RIGHT OF THE HEAVEN OF FORM

I live my right to self-acceptance and self-love now.
I know that I am worthy of my own love at all times.
God always loves me, as do His angels.

The Heaven of Creation

The second level of heaven is known as the Heaven of Creation.
It contains the spiritual powerful forces of the Dynamis, Virtues
and Dominions. These beings work in the Heart Chakra to bring
us deeper experiences of love, trust, hope and joy.

They encourage us to develop sustainable love relationships
that will nourish us throughout our life. They want us to fill the
heart center with the pure energy of love, joy and peace. This is
done by building harmonious relationships that support our
growth and well-being, that honor the truth of us as individuals
and that hold us through the trials, losses, and traumas we will
sustain as humans.

These angelic beings set in motion the forces that enhance
our ability to receive and give love. They help us love ourselves, in
all our various guises. They teach us how to accept and love
others, without falling into criticism or reactivity. Learning how to
love life is what opens the doors to the Heaven of Creation.

These three forces, who thrive in this heaven, allow love to flow easily into all aspects of our lives. They teach us to ask for the love we need, and to find the work and creative expressions that demonstrate our love. Their whole purpose is to bring love fully into our lives. They help us access love, assimilate love, digest love, and give love as part of our spiritual path.

In this level of heaven our being thrives where love lives, deep within our hearts. We are asked to seek work we love, be with people we love, do what we love. It is an opportunity to find fulfillment and true intimacy. It is a very high level of personal empowerment to access this level of heaven.

These three angelic forces want us to learn the nature of love, see it develop and grow within us and receive our fill of it through the things we do, and the people we share ourselves with.

In this level of heaven, individuals take responsibility for the love they call to themselves. They learn to live in love as the creative medium of all life. Initiations are all about being able to love and to forgive. This is the level where gratitude is affirmed as the essential ingredient in all experiences. We show gratitude for those who are in our lives, and those who have gone before us to pave the way for our experiences to unfold.

These angelic forces attempt to teach us to love ourselves first and then reach out to others in love. They know that we are only capable of sustained love when we love and accept ourselves. Their job is to foster the pursuit of personal happiness and help us trust in love.

When we are lost or have been wounded by a loss or lack of love these forces help us heal, regain our desire to love again and send us back into the world to re-formulate healthy relationships and creative projects that will build confidence in ourselves.

The Dominions and the Heart Chakra

The Dominions develop love for others that is transpersonal in nature. In other words, they train us to love humanity in general, and to honor life in all creatures for no reason other than the joy of loving. This includes loving strangers, children, animals, nature, and the world around us. It teaches us acceptance, and releases criticism, competition and any sense of superiority that can take us from our spiritual development.

This keeps our hearts open to love. It is not personal but it does work deep within us to show compassion and understanding for our fellow travelers on the path of light. It also teaches us to look at what separates us from one another and what stops love flowing between us. When we love impersonally our heart center is open to the goodness and sweetness of life. It places us in a relationship with life itself.

The Dominions open our heart to the joy of life. In that place we are best able to choose what we love to do, where we want to do it and how we want to do what makes our heart sing. When we have this attitude we are responsible for the great adventure that unfolds as we step out into life on the platform of love.

We can accomplish many things if we are willing to approach our life from this perspective. The Dominions are indiscriminate about how we choose to love just so long as we do so. If we are ever resistant to openly loving they will show us people who, in spite of handicaps, accidents, or lack of resources, have a smile on their faces and are moving forward without self-pity or blame.

These encounters open us to the truth that we are blessed and have, in reality, little to complain about and much to love. Gratitude for life is the foundational truth of these angelic beings.

Dominions keep the heart fuels burning and open us to a

greater capacity to experience personal intimacy and love with another. They remind us constantly of the need to stop our frantic behavior and smell the roses. They ask us to find beauty in people and nature that is all around us and to simply enjoy life. We feel their spirits strongly at rock concerts, sports events, and large assemblies where people gather in a spirit of joy and celebration. We feel them in the woods, by the seaside and wherever nature shines her beauty and bounty upon us.

The Virtues and the Heart Chakra

The Virtues are the angelic beings who cultivate our inner forces of wisdom. They inspire us to become givers in life. They enable us, through one means or another, to choose to give back to life. They provide us with skills of discernment and they guide us through the portals of knowledge to choose what path will best reflect our talents and gifts back into the world. They teach us to anchor our abilities in the best ways that will serve us and serve others at the same time. Loving what we do is the best way to insure that our gifts will find full expression and give us deep satisfaction. The Virtues help develop our inner knowing about universal truths through doing what we love. We learn about boundaries, the principles of engagement and the best way to express ourselves because we want to protect what we do and keep at it for as long as possible.

When we love what we do we learn to take care of ourselves, eat properly, get enough rest, make wise choices about what we want and where we will go because we want to insure that we can continue to do what we love.

Built into the experience of doing what we love is loving ourselves so we can continue to do what we love. It's interesting that when we cease to love what we do we stop taking care of ourselves, sometimes becoming depressed or ill. People who love what they do have the capacity to give time, money and energy to continuing to do what they love.

The Virtues keep the heart forces balanced between taking in what we need for our health and well-being and giving in a way that can be sustained by the forces of the world. The Virtues show us how to balance and manage all activities that require our energy and attention. They watch to see that we can defend ourselves against the onslaught of those who would diminish our efforts.

The Virtues work deep within the heart to help us cultivate a wisdom linked with the heart. They tell us it is fine to be happy doing what we love and their hope is that we will do it well. They are helping us to dream of how we might serve the world in better and better ways and from a more loving place. This is great wisdom they provide to all on the path of love.

The Dynamis and the Heart Chakra

The Dynamis stimulate the imaginative forces that allow us to see ourselves well loved by another. They want us to feel we are loved and supported by friends, a significant other, or by people who simply cherish us and want the best for us. When we know we are loved we act from our heart, we learn to give to others and we learn that infinite dimensions of love exist in life. They want us to know love in many different forms as we mature and develop.

The Dynamis build the forces of loyalty, constancy and courage within the heart field to help us deal with the perils of relationships and the problems we can encounter when we are intimately involved with others. They know that love can only exist within the foundation of these qualities. If it is going to be strong and enduring we must learn how to relate without falling into the need to be right, condemn others for their choices or impose our will on them.

The Dynamis help us establish the rhythms and cycles of healing and transformation that help us grow into the ability to sustain a good relationship. They supply the heart with the cosmic forces of love and it is up to us to know how to channel these forces so that love endures.

They bring humanity the music of the spheres so that poetry, mathematics and music inspire the muse in each of us to love more fully and with care. They stimulate the loving heart of people to be better, grow and mature and always be the loving friend, partner, child, parent, sister or brother we know we are. They encourage us to be love itself.

All three categories of angelic being teach us to love ourselves and accept others as they are. This is a truth of the heart in the fullness of love. As we love ourselves and accept the responsibilities that come with loving others we grow into our own magnificence. We become the love we give. We transcend our limitations, we grow spiritually and we are deeply embraced by these angelic beings of love.

At the same time, they encourage us to move through whatever beliefs stop us from knowing real love to come into relationship with others. They help us dispel any fears that make us shy or timid to reach out to another. They bring friends into our lives who love us for who we are. They mend relationships that have been rent by misunderstandings and need another chance to flourish.

They want our hearts to be strong, resilient, and capable of great love for many years of our life.

They teach each person that they have the heart of an angel and can love, protect and bring healing to the world through the relationships they foster. They reside deep within the inner chambers of the heart, reminding us we are love itself and all we need do is give that love in all encounters, and call to us those people who will allow us to love them fully and unconditionally.

They remind us we have the capacity to be loving and gentle individuals, expressing the truth of ourselves as God's children. They tell us that if God can love us to such a degree then we can love others in the same way. Believing that love draws us to itself we will walk across burning coals and through strange territory to encounter those who we are asked to love.

MEDITATION ON THE HEAVEN OF CREATION

Sit quietly and take several deep breaths. Release any areas of tension you may have that disturb your reflections. Breathe into these areas and release the tension. Begin to meditate on the three aspects of love in the Heaven of Creation. Perhaps you can see a pattern emerging. As we develop our capacity to love, our levels of responsibility increase with regard to the quality of our actions, the clarity of our thoughts and our way of being with others.

Each level of the Heaven of Creation asks that we become more loving, more giving, more understanding. We have built into this level of heaven all the angelic forces who can guide us through the perils of love. They teach us to love life, to do what we love and to draw to us relationships that sustain us in love.

We are capable of this level of inner development. It requires time and an understanding that we are imperfect beings striving to achieve an ideal. There will be times when it is challenging to love humanity and times when we have difficulties with our work, no matter how much we love what we do. Building relationships that allow us to love and be loved is probably the most challenging of all these three aspects of love.

Patience demands that we take our time, think about ascending to higher levels of personal responsibility and choose healing and wholeness as we step into this realm of heaven. We learn this is what we have come to earth to do and these angelic forces are willing to be our teachers. Choose love in all aspects of living and experience the peace, tenderness, and sweetness it brings into your life.

PRAYER

Beloved angelic beings of the Heaven of Creation, thank you for the opportunity to experience the joys of love. I am learning to grasp the essential nature of love as I engage with life. I ask you to support me in choosing love. Help my desire for love to be stronger than my desire to separate, condemn, criticize and destroy any possibilities of love blossoming and growing.

I affirm love as the foundation of my life. It is the first
cause of all that I am and all that I do.

THE RIGHT OF THE HEAVEN OF CREATION

I accept my right to love and to be loved.

The Heaven of Paradise

The highest level of heaven is called the Heaven of Paradise. It
is the one closest to God and the place where we manifest our
greatest dreams, highest hopes and deepest longings. It is here
that we are absolutely responsible for creating the life we say
we want.

The angelic forces that reside in this level of heaven work at
the most profound level of consciousness. They are known as
the Seraphim, Cherubim, and the Thrones. These powerful
beings exist in the realm of pure consciousness and are associated
with the upper chakras. They resonate in the Throat Chakra, the
Brow Chakra and the Crown Chakra.

They also contain the spiritual forces of the Christ Light and
the power of the Holy Spirit. The Blessed Virgin Mary, great
feminine archetype of the Mother of Us All and Mother of God
resides in this realm of heaven as well.

Here these holy forces receive our petitions and act upon our
requests. Our resonance with them is energetic and spiritual.
They all surround the throne of God singing praise and glory of
the Most High throughout eternity.

These forces work within us as clear channels for focused thought. They inspire us to our greatest acts and transform the residue of unconsciousness into healing and love. They help us form our words, think our thoughts and bond with those who are the focus of love and desire.

They teach us, above all else, that we are worthy of a fulfilled, happy life, replete with prosperity, pleasure, fun and joy. They help us reach the gates of paradise in our lives. They know we can be rich in spirit at all times and that we don't have to suffer to experience this. They encourage us to visualize our highest good at all times.

Their greatest strength to humanity is to remind us God is One. There is only one Source and all things come from God. If God is the living presence and is for our well-being and good, who could stand against us? We are reminded that we have the ability to create our lives and define for ourselves what paradise is for us. We do this in a fully conscious and careful way that includes all possibilities for joy, health, prosperity, creativity, unity and oneness to manifest in our lives.

These angelic forces support our inner growth and maturity so that we can create what will serve us best and, at the same time, bring healing to the world. At a certain point in our spiritual development we will seek to attain this high level of self-mastery. We are asked to know the truth of who we are and that all we seek comes to us because of who we are, children of the One God.

The Seraphim and the Throat Chakra

The Seraphim live in the Heaven of Paradise and work within the energy of the Throat Chakra. They bring God's love into communities and fellowships throughout the world as the full, conscious expression of truth, will, communication, and creative energy.

The Seraphim teach us to love one another as one people, one planet. They live within the ears, which hear, the mouth, which tastes, the nose, which smells, and the throat, which speaks to all humanity. They awaken when we have passed through our initiations into love. They emerge as expressions of oneness and a voice that strikes the chord of peace, truth and integrity.

They are intricately linked with our senses and, particularly, our ability to speak our truth. So much of our truth has been swallowed through years of suppression. We learn to speak what is expected of us, seldom feeling strong enough in our being to express the truth we experience. We are not educated to allow people to share their deep feelings or raise questions about the mystery of life. Somehow these have been denied us and the Throat Chakra begins to atrophy after 50.

When this happens the entire facial structure becomes congested. It is said that sinus problems are the accumulation of self-pity materialized into clogged mucus in our sinus cavities. Running noses, congested throats and ears are all signs of suppression. All addictions pass through the narrow passage of the throat and we become weakened vessels for the truth to express itself through us.

Opening up the Throat Chakra requires the help of the Seraphim. They are so strong and powerful that when they stand behind us we have the courage to speak from our heart, to share our ideas and truths. They encourage us to always shout out our affirmations, saying "YES" to life in a bold, loud voice. They want us to affirm ourselves, affirm our lives and feel that we have the power to express what we know to be true.

The Seraphim teach us how to work together with the gift of clear communication for the greater good. They have blessed us with the outpouring of God's love through the healing power of song, the written word and all forms of creative expression. They remind us that it is the Word of God that transforms our life and bring us healing. When we say "YES" to life, God is speaking through us.

Seraphim are known as the spirits of truth. Their light resonates through us whenever we are living, speaking and sharing our truth. We always have a choice to speak clearly and link our words to our heart. They help us form our phrases so that we do not damage others. The truth can be harsh when it is not connected to the heart forces and they act as that bridge between the coldness of the mind and the warmth of the heart. These angelic beings seek only to communicate in love, with love and through love.

We hear them in the songs we sing, the poetry we recite, the babble of children playing, babies crying, lovers cooing and anyone asking for help. The Seraphim are the bridge to connect us with others. They represent the forces of creative expression because they let us speak our desires out loud. When this happens life is more beautiful because of it.

These are the forces that strengthen the Throat Chakra. They allow us to use our will and act from it. They teach us to hear the nuances of truth that someone dares to speak. When our throat is open and energy is flowing we are allowing life to truly run like a deep river through us. The throat expresses our joy, our sorrow, our pleasure and our hopes. It holds the key to the deepest satisfaction when it functions in integrity and expresses in truth.

The Cherubim and the Brow Chakra

The Cherubim are known as the spirits of harmony. They live within the Brow Chakra which is the control center. This is where all other energy forces are synthesized and come together to create understanding and intelligence.

The Cherubim bring balance and healing to wounds of separation and loss. They also help us create a clear vision of our heart's desire for happiness. They help us think out what would make us happy, give us pleasure and deepen our trust in God as the living presence within us.

They help us see the power of forgiveness to release what we have been attached to and what has weighted our spirits down. Once we are sure that we are ready to forgive they help us release the stagnant energy of resentment and anger.

They want us current in life so that we can move forward, create and manifest our ideas of paradise. Without them working in us we could be cold and embittered people remembering every insult, hurt and loss. They serve to eliminate the weight that anger carries in our field. It also draws negative experiences that keep us locked in fear, lack and loss.

As we align our hearts to the power of love, peace and joy we want this to be what our life is rich in at all times. To live with a sense of sufficiency; to know all is well all the time, and that we are loved by God and all His angels is paradise.

The Cherubim keep our spirits positive through the act of forgiveness and the process of creative visioning to see what the spirit seeks out as its next step in development. As we release we also create. This is what helps us become empowered souls. They free the heart of pain and keep our spirits open to goodness.

The Cherubim bring harmony and in this place we choose

more love, more joy, more pleasure, more delight and greater degrees of personal happiness. They help us put an end to suffering through the insight they bring us. They defy the forces of stubbornness, criticism and doubt and are so strong that when they work within our Brow Chakra we know we only want to live intelligently and lovingly in the world, surrounded by love and filled with joy.

The Thrones and the Crown Chakra

The Thrones are the highest angelic beings in creation. They are closest to the Divine Throne of God and are known as the spirits of will. They transform weaknesses into courage, pain into healing and suffering into grace. They see us through the challenges and initiations that bring us to this level of heaven. They give us the forces of will to soldier through the difficult times of our life and remind us that "this too shall pass" and we will find love and joy. They keep the love of life burning in our hearts as they teach us that we have the will to surmount most obstacles.

This level of heaven exists beyond conflict and doubt. This is the realm of pure love and joy. It manifests in all our heart's desires where we experience unity, wholeness and ease in our lives. Things come about easily because we are at one with God. We do not have anything that separates us from living our good.

The Thrones have forged the strength of will to create the deepest spiritual connection with Source we, as human beings, can possibly experience. This is where we experience complete unity with God and know there is only the One, indivisible Source from which all things come. As we connect with this, forgive others, show gratitude for our lives, our connection becomes immediate and manifestation is instant.

At this level of consciousness we formulate our thoughts about how we want to participate in life. Are we givers, do we bring healing to others, is our manner one that tells the world all is well? We claim our good and we then allow the forces of the Thrones to bring into form all that we need to live our life according to our will.

The Thrones live within the Crown Chakra where we hold the Christ Light that burns brightly in us. It is the eternal light that shines through all circumstances. It helps us bury our dead, welcome the newborn, bless young lovers, and celebrate life for all.

The Thrones bring the awareness that life itself is a great celebration and we are all invited to the party. We can rejoice in the knowledge that we are so loved by God that we can work together in Him to construct our lives according to truth, right action, peace, love and beauty. We can claim and include all the other qualities of goodness God shows us as our own.

The Forces of the Angels

We can call upon those forces for good any time and any place we feel we need help, want clarity and have need of their power and assistance. They bring us our good, shower us with their love, and soothe our pain. They help us move on in life towards a deeper understanding of the mystery, and a greater love for ourselves and all mankind. They remove from our life and consciousness what is unwholesome and no longer serves us. They teach us to be discerning, and make good choices rich in love and joy. They manifest as our ability to forgive, release, and find our way to love.

MEDITATION

Sit comfortably and take several deep breaths. Scan your body for areas of tension. Breathe into these areas and release the tension. Begin to think about what heaven on earth would look like for you. Can you visualize your idea of paradise? Would your world be filled with the joys of love, the pleasures that delight you, the people you care about and the projects you most desire to fulfill? Would there be abundant prosperity, comfort, beauty and a great sense of peace and accomplishment?

Visualize exactly what you would like to experience in your realm of paradise. Would you be willing to grow and mature, give up your anger and hatred, forgive and release everyone who ever hurt or troubled you in order to have this? Would you be willing to trust God sufficiently that you could believe this level of joy and happiness could be yours to enjoy and partake in?

The whole idea of paradise is one that sages and mystics saw as being a part of another world. They could not see past the torment and misery of life to envision it as something each individual is capable of creating out of the endless supply of good God bestows on His universe.

Allow yourself to feel, even momentarily, that bliss is within grasp and all you have to do is grow your spirit into it. If you are willing to be the Source within your life and know truly that all good comes from within you can have your vision of paradise.

PRAYER FOR THE ANGELS OF THE
HEAVEN OF PARADISE

Beloved angelic beings, I pray to you for the faith
I need to know that heaven on earth is a possibility
I can embrace. I am willing to work through my
fears, doubts and cynical beliefs that embody my
sense of separation. I claim unity, wholeness, joy,
pleasure, love, prosperity and health as my birthright
as a child of God. I know Source is within me.
Help me accept my good, and enjoy my realm of
paradise totally.

AFFIRMATION

I affirm the wonders of paradise are mine
to have and enjoy!

THE RIGHT OF THE HEAVEN OF PARADISE

I claim my right to perfection now.

CHAPTER 4

Developing the Spiritual Tools for Connecting With the Angels

We all need a way to enhance our spiritual connection with God and the angelic realm. Although the simplest prayers are "Please help me!" and "Thank you," there is more we can do to develop and fortify our bond with spirit.

The following tools are designed to support your access to the angelic realms. They can help you connect easily and effortlessly. What is asked of you is that you be willing to cultivate a practice that can be done as part of your daily routine. Then when you need access quickly you will experience it immediately because you have already put it in place.

These tools calm the spirit, quiet the mind and open the channel for hearing the wise guidance of your life that angels bring. They are ancient techniques, used since the beginning of time, when man felt he had to reconnect with his spiritual roots. They are literally thousands of years old and used in every culture in the history of the world.

In order for these tools to work for you they do require regular practice and a willingness, on your part, to make the connection.

Be patient, take time out of your busy daily life to practice them on a regular basis. This discipline will pay off as you feel more secure within yourself, and assured that all is well in your world. You will experience peace, profound joy and the depths of an internal connection with Source. Practice leads to the fruits of your efforts.

Meditation

Meditation is an ancient tool used to empty the mind so that the deep connection with spirit can be experienced. You clear your mind of its clutter of information, impressions and ideas in the stillness of your being. You are tapping into a deep well of spirit which is a real part of yourself.

This experience of inner peace allows the portals to open the channel for you to receive higher knowledge, spiritual guidance and unconditional love. It is always there with us, and, in truth, never leaves us for a moment. However, we are often so focused outside ourselves onto the world around us that we need to stop for regular intervals to turn the tide of consciousness inward to God.

Meditation is the practice of slowing the mind, disengaging the senses, and calming the nerves. In other words, you "flip the switch" and turn your awareness inward. This is where you will experience God. As you turn your awareness away from the outer world and shift your awareness towards your inner world you will experience freedom, love, delight and energy that will fill your being.

As we transcend our thoughts and emotions we move into the true silence that envelops the Divine Presence living within us. This is when the quiet, strong inner voice of angels speaks and, if we are awake, we listen in joy and gratitude.

Meditation turns the stillness into consciousness itself. If you have difficulty concentrating on stilling and quieting the mind focus your attention on your breath. This helps focus your mind and it releases thoughts, relaxes tension and keeps your awareness in the present moment. It is a good way to disengage your attention from the daily drama of life.

Meditation is traditionally done in a sitting position. However, it can be done moving, running or dancing. Moving meditations allow us to experience the stillness of our inner world within the context of the dynamic world of movement. For many people this is a very good way to make the internal connections.

Meditation helps us formulate clear and positive thoughts. These thoughts can lead to good intentions to transform some aspect of your life. When these intentions come from the depths of your spirit they bring with them the force of will needed to implement new ideas.

Meditation keeps us open to the realm of possibilities from where love, healing and joy emanate. It lets us define our boundaries, assess our likes and dislikes and experience the truth of who we are without judgment, criticism or punishment.

At the same time, meditation allows us to realize we are an expression of God designed in our unique individuality. This gives us the possibility of knowing we are united with all life. Meditation creates mental detachment, emotional balance and inner peace. It also lets us send love, peace and healing to the world and to bless our lives.

If you have never tried meditation or have been too agitated to sit still for any period of time it is best to begin with a few minutes daily till you relax enough to increase your time. It is not a contest or a competition. It is, truly, an opportunity to quiet your mind, take time out and be with the Divine.

Affirmative Prayer

Prayer acknowledges God as Source. We pray to ask for help, petition for healing and, also, to give thanks. Prayer is our plea for good to come; be it for ourselves or those we love. Each prayer is heard and answered. It may not come in the form we expect but it is always held in the Divine arms of God and acknowledged in its own way.

Affirmative prayer acknowledges God as Source within us. It affirms our ability to claim our good by seeing it as already in existence. This means we see prosperity, we see health, we see love as something already manifested in our mind's eye. We use our prayer to say thank you for that which we seek. It affirms through our faith that it is ours to claim now.

We pray for what we want, knowing that it is ours. This can be better health, greater prosperity and abundance, deep and meaningful love, or help with any situation in our lives. By seeing it we create the template that will allow God to fill our lives with what we claim. We see what we ask for as accomplished and already ours.

Praying as if our petition has been granted, with thanks and gratitude, gives us our power to create our life as we would like it to be. As we ascend closer to the Heaven of Paradise we learn to envision our desires and take full responsibility for our good.

The real work comes, not in the prayer, but in having the faith that it is already ours. Our prayer is already known in the mind and heart of God and in that template it has already been given. When we know it as ours then all victimhood, martyrdom and servitude are released because we take our power of creation back into our hands and stop projecting it out into the ethers to a disembodied God.

When we accept the truth that God is the living presence within us we become more conscious of our ability to create and manifest our intentions. We choose the good because we know it can and will come into being. We choose what will make our hearts sing because we can have that which we desire.

The universal force we acknowledge as God responds to all positive intentions. We claim our good as if it were already accomplished. We rest in the faith that what has been requested is now answered. We live as if this were so now.

The universal force, or God, only knows how to say "YES." When we say, for example, "I am poor and unhappy!" the universal life force says "YES." When we say, for example, "I am thriving and happy!" the universal life force says "YES." That is what it does. If we claim something to be our truth now, the universe can only respond affirmatively.

The more responsibility we take for what we desire now the easier it is for the universe to bring our prayer into physical reality. At each level of heaven we find that the angels require us to be more responsible for our heart's desires. They see us grow from the spiritual children of God to the responsible and mature adults of God who claim their good now.

God is neither punishing nor harsh; it is love itself. Our limitations, judgments and doubts are what keep us victims and make God responsible for our lives. By opening our consciousness to the angelic realm we can pray affirmatively to receive our good. As this manifests we can grow into the truth of who we are. We can become more adept at inseminating our world with love, joy and peace so we can experience those qualities in our own life. This is how the grace of the Holy Spirit serves humanity. As we mature and grow into our spiritual powers our lives become the answered prayers.

This form of prayer honors us as co-creators with God for the quality and beauty of our life. It empowers us by acknowledging our desires for a richer and better life. It is our faith that makes this attainable. Through our prayers of gratitude, we live in the peace of knowing all is well. Saying "Thank you, God, for all I claim for myself now," is a gracious prayer for each and every blessing we have.

This form of prayer is based on knowing God is loving and benign. God and His Angels only want to see us happy and fulfilled. If we want the same for ourselves we do the work, find the time to cultivate an attitude of gratitude, step into our power of creation and watch the good begin to manifest.

Affirmative prayer sees the sick as whole, the drunk as sober, the sinner as redeemed and, in that unique way, it works. It sets the template before our Father to see what wants to be realized. It has no expectations, nor judgment, nor time-specific time frame. The more we repeat our prayers the stronger this template for good becomes.

Affirmative prayer allows us to see the best for ourselves and claim our good now. It offers infinite gratitude for the good that takes place in our lives. It releases the negative, forgets the past, and dismisses all condemning judgment. We call this "letting go and letting God."

Begin to practice this and see what results it brings. Take time, be patient and allow the good to find its way into your life. Do not judge it, or criticize it. Bless it as it comes and enjoy what is given. Allow more of your good to find you every day and you will revel in your blessings. Angels will smile with you, laugh in your delight and you will experience happiness at the power of your ability to call to you the joy you seek.

EXAMPLE OF AFFIRMATIVE PRAYER

I know there is One God in which I live, breathe and have my being. God lives in me, as me and through me. In this knowing I claim my good now. I know all good comes to me because of who I am. As a child of God my desire is to claim love, peace, joy, health, prosperity, fulfillment, pleasure, ease and creativity for myself now. I know that the truth of me gladly receives these gifts now and I am deeply grateful for the wonder and magnificence of God to realize my requests now. I release this to the Universal life force that flows through everything to go out into Creation and come back to me as my desire manifested.

I pray for peace in the world, healing for all and ask that each person I love and know finds their joy now.

In the awareness that this is manifesting now I affirm: AND SO IT IS.

Affirmations

Affirmations are positive statements of intent that affirm our good. They are always said in the present tense and affirm what we wish and hope to experience in a loud, declarative voice. They serve the purpose of making our intentions for good a loud, definitive and focused statement. They keep our mind clearly anchored in the possibility of good. They make the negative thoughts around our desires a reminder of how we easily sabotage what we want.

Affirmations teach us how to reject our negative thinking by being aware of it and how it creeps into our minds. Each time this happens we can say to ourselves, "Thank you for reminding me how negative I can be." It is important to know that even the negative serves a purpose.

Affirmations teach us to claim our good now. As we affirm our worth, honor our choices for love and let spirit take us forward into life we keep proclaiming the power of creation each step of the way. We release all negativity that comes up around our affirmations and we keep focusing on what we desire.

Affirmations are said in the present tense, as if we were living the truth of our desires now. For example: "I am grateful and blessed by the sweetness of love." "I have all the love I need." "I am prospering now." "I affirm that money comes to me from all directions."

Affirmations can be repeated many times throughout the day. They are best said when we are doubtful, unsure or afraid because they remind us to claim our good now. They can be written down or said out loud. They can be said in front of a mirror or said silently. They remind us we can create heaven on earth each time we affirm ourselves.

Affirmations create an energetic field that attracts to us what we claim for ourselves. Affirmations are worth practicing because they force our mind to consider the realm of positive choices available to us. They keep us looking at the good we want, rather than what we don't have. They engage the will by making the mind affirmative.

Practice doing affirmations. Write them down and put them on the wall or mirror. Say them to yourself several times a day. As your good begins to manifest take time to be grateful for what you receive.

Some examples of affirmations:

I am grateful for all the good that I receive.

I affirm love fills my life.

Prosperity and abundance are my birthright.
I claim them now.

I enjoy perfect health and beauty.

Goodness comes to me through everyone
I meet today.

I am grounded in the truth of my being.
I know who I am.

I am happy, fulfilled and creative. I have everything
I need to life in sufficiency.

All is well and all is well and all is well.

Thank you, God, for the joy and wonder of my life.
I am so blessed.

Reflective Practice

Reflective practice comes out of the work of two British nurses who had a need to step back from their engagement with patients and reflect on the best way to understand their needs. It has grown into a spiritual practice for many health practitioners. Its principles can be easily understood and it is very helpful in grasping the deeper realities of life as it expresses through the people and situations in our life.

This is an excellent tool for asking the questions that lead to insight about any situation, relationship or person we need more clarity about. It offers insights that allow us to look deeper than the surface. In reflective practice we take time to focus our attention on a situation or person. We ask questions that lead us towards greater understanding and deeper insight.

By stepping back and looking at a person, situation or event, with clarity and detachment, we reap a harvest of wisdom and information. We also do not become engaged in their story but can see more clearly what would support them or help them heal. This allows us to make wholesome choices for compassion, kindness and love.

Often the questions are simple. "What is this situation about in my life?" or "What is it I need to learn that will help me relate to this person in a more loving way?" When we ask, we wait quietly for the answer to emerge. We do not push or assume we know the answer. We accept what comes into our minds and we work with that until we have resolution and clarification.

It may be useful to keep a journal where you describe the situation and write down your questions along with the answers you receive. Review them from time to time and see what patterns emerge over a period of time. See if your guidance was useful and helped the person or situation come to a higher level of well-being.

Reflection allows angels to whisper in our ears and reveal truths to us. These can keep our minds open and ease our fears and tensions. They can help us do the smart thing in a situation, or resolve our inner turmoil and conflicts easily and readily. Reflection is a balance between action and passivity. It is the in-between place where we seek clarity and truth before we move into action. It can save us the embarrassment of assuming something that may not be real and it can carry us into the realm of healing a situation or relationship.

Reflective practice requires that we look carefully at a situation and wait for our guidance to direct us appropriately. The questions can be simple, such as:

"What is the best way forward in this relationship with my sister?" The answer may be simple as well. "Be gentle and don't push her. She can make her own choices for her life. When you love her you support her choices."

Regarding a situation that may be challenging you can ask: "What do I do in this financial crisis to get through without loss or debt?" The answer may be "Listen carefully to what your needs are. Spend your money on things that give you joy and pleasure. Trust in your good and that you are here doing what best serves the world. Allow your good to come to you now."

Reflective practice can be about anything you need to focus your attention on to make your life easier and happier. Ask the questions you need to receive your guidance. Angels love helping you move through any situation, empowered and in control of yourself. They come very close to us when we ask for help.

The Power of Spiritual Tools

These tools can help us cultivate a healthy inner guidance system that we can rely on in times of stress or concern. They allow us to access the higher powers of the angelic realm to work with us, help us and guide us forward. They help us enjoy well-being, joy and fulfillment. They connect us to the depths of our wisdom and truth. They give the angels the opportunity to speak to us and be the official guides for our happiness. This truth is expressed in Psalm 91, which says:

> He who dwells in the shelter of the Most High
> will rest in the shadow of the Almighty.

> I will say of the Lord, "He is my refuge and my
> fortress, my God, in whom I trust."

> Surely he will save you from the fowler's snare
> and from the deadly pestilence.

> He will cover you with his feathers,
> and under his wings you will find refuge;
> his faithfulness will be your shield and rampart.

> You will not fear the terror of night,
> nor the arrow that flies by day,

> nor the pestilence that stalks in the darkness,
> nor the plague that destroys at midday.

> A thousand may fall at your side,
> ten thousand at your right hand,
> but it will not come near you.

> You will only observe with your eyes
> and see the punishment of the wicked.

> If you make the Most High your dwelling –
> even the Lord, who is my refuge –

then no harm will befall you,
no disaster will come near your tent.

For he will command his angels concerning you
to guard you in all your ways;

they will lift you up in their hands,
so that you will not strike your foot against a stone.

You will tread upon the lion and the cobra;
you will trample the great lion and the serpent.

"Because he loves me," says the Lord, "I will rescue
    him;
I will protect him, for he acknowledges my name.

He will call upon me, and I will answer him;
I will be with him in trouble,
I will deliver him and honor him.

With long life will I satisfy him
and show him my salvation."

PART 2

CHAKRAS AND ANGELS

INTRODUCTION

The angels address our challenges, help us resolve our personal issues and encourage us to strive for inner growth. They support us through life's initiations into higher levels of consciousness.

They work directly within our energy system to bring balance and healing to the chakras. As we develop inner strength and cultivate wisdom we gain a better understanding of life's mysteries. In our maturity we have a more wholesome sense of what love is, how gratitude blesses us and self-worth comes out of the truth of our being. Much reveals itself to us through angels awakening our spirit.

We develop spiritual maturity every time we tell ourselves the truth about our feelings. When we stop punishing ourselves for our imperfections we heal what is harsh and punishing in us. This is how we realize our wholeness. Angels strive to help us with this by showering us with love. Our spirit expands in the love and joy they bless us with.

Angelic beings carry our spirit when our load is light; they carry it when it is heavy. They are constant, true and dependable. They are there when we are vulnerable, frightened and unsure. They are there when we celebrate a victory over the obstacles in our path.

When we experience how loved and supported we truly are by the spiritual realm it frees us to let go of tension and fear. Being grateful and acknowledging angels is our way of saying we are aware of their efforts on our behalf. We could not overcome anything on our own.

The angelic realm assures us all is well; they remind us we are never alone or without recourse for help. They love to see us ascend to new levels of self-love and truth on our path to paradise.

The angels work with us by using the chakras as the conduit for universal life energy. They work to keep our channels open to receiving our highest good through these centers. The chakras funnel this life force into our body, through our emotions and into our thoughts. This energy is the fuel for our consciousness. There is no life without it.

When we live in fear or doubt, or willfully refuse our good then this energy becomes blocked and stagnant. It slows down. If we are hateful and angry, depressed or anxious, the system becomes deeply imbalanced. What keeps this system fluid is physical activity, emotional expression, positive thoughts and spiritual insights. This energy moves through all levels of being.

The Chakras and Attitudes

As long as we are physically alive the life force flows through our bodies and works in our energy centers. The intensity and quality of that energy is dependent on our thinking and feeling, and, of course, our lifestyle. As we release negativity that flow increases. When we affirm our lives and love ourselves the flow increases.

If we persist in holding onto old ideas that are not in alignment with our highest good we weigh our spirit down and eventually weaken the field. If we move towards positive thinking that acknowledges God as the living Source within us then we claim our good easily and effortlessly, because the power to create lives within us. This will be expressed by higher levels of love and self-expression, joy, health and prosperity. This is what is meant by claiming our good.

Angels conduct the life force into and through the chakras. It will automatically slow down the flow when we are stuck with a limited or negative belief that dams the flow, especially any thought that invalidates our value. From their viewpoint, looking at us from the inside out, the angels know there is always another, more loving way to look at ourselves, or a situation.

When we look from a higher place we expand our vision and open our hearts to our own shortcomings. We learn to be gentle and kind to ourselves. This helps us find a more compassionate and loving way of treating ourselves. It stops the conflict and eliminates the punishment we can perpetrate against ourselves for not being perfect.

Angels support us through all our challenges, regardless of our choices. Their hope is that we can keep our consciousness awake and expand our ability to receive more of the good. We are always loved, always cared for and always treated kindly and gently by these great forces who work on our behalf at every turn.

They encourage us to make right choices for good. They want us to claim our happiness, health, prosperity, and love each moment. They do, however, honor whatever choices we make without punishment or judgment. We are the only ones capable of transforming our ideas about ourselves.

Energy has no qualitative distinctions. It flows through the chakras regardless of age, size, race, or intelligence. The only thing that does limit it is how we express our selves in acts of love and by acknowledging the good with gratitude. When we forgive those who have hurt us, for instance, more energy flows in our centers. They become less congested.

By the same token, when we affirm our worth and honor our choices for love then these channels expand and open more fully. How much energy we have flowing through us is dependent on our beliefs and attitudes. Angels just wait at the portals of consciousness ready to bring to us what we call to ourselves.

In the physical body this energy feeds the organs and controls the ductless glands that secrete hormones. At an energetic level, in the etheric body, this energy flow regulates vitality, immunity and emotions. In the astral and egoic bodies this flow controls the thinking processes and our spiritual awareness.

As we move from the Root Chakra, located at the base of the spine, to the Crown Chakra, located at the top of the head, this energy flow becomes more refined as does its use. The quality of the energy becomes finer and lighter. The energy we require for our physical body is different than what is used for our mental and spiritual needs.

Our Belief System

Beliefs that limit our experiences and awareness limit our life. These beliefs can have their roots in gender, family, tribal, and community consciousness. They may have been created to insure survival during times of hardship and duress over many generations. Questioning whether these beliefs have validity in our life today is what transforms our life force from old, tired energy to a living presence of vitality, truth and love.

Questioning whether our beliefs serve us is a healing process that requires a willingness to go within and ask: "Is this good, is this true, is this right for me now?" When we look at our beliefs we begin harvesting out the negativity which is fear, doubt, harshness and punishment for being less than perfect. This is what makes our energy expand and gives us health.

If, for example, we believe life is hard, or that no one loves us, or that we are unworthy, our energy will be heavy and limited.

We will experience recurring breakdowns where we crash and manifest poor health, unhappiness and depression.

As we affirm our worth, release the shame and guilt that weigh us down, we honor more healthy choices for love and happiness. We expand our energy flow and, with that, bring in more of our good.

We find it easier to express our creativity, live in loving relationships, and have success with our projects. When we are in the flow of life we affirm our good, and express joy in all that we do. We experience fulfillment.

The more we release self-limiting beliefs the faster we retrieve our energy. This is the alchemical transmutation of lead into gold, or negativity into consciousness. This gives us a clearer and higher vision of our lives.

The pay-off for being congruent with our inner reality is that we become more vibrant and healthy. This is age-defying, soul-enhancing and intellectually stimulating. Angels say yes to this and hope we are willing to live this reality now.

The Rights of Each Chakra

Each chakra has an archetypal right related to its function. These rights define the optimal expression and fulfillment of each energy center. The rights are expanded and enhanced through meditation, prayer, reflection and affirmation. Meditating on each right fortifies the chakra and strengthens that right in our mind as something worthy of attaining.

It allows the angels of that chakra to give us the best of their love. Their job is to expand our awareness and open us to healing what has been wounded in the process of growth.

The rights of each chakra are as follows, start[...]
the spine and working up to the Crown:

- The Root Chakra's right is to live your own life.
- The Sacral Chakra's right is to experience pleasure, health, prosperity and creativity.
- The Solar Plexus's right is to know your value, have self-respect, self-esteem, confidence, empowerment and freedom of choice.
- The Heart Chakra's right is to love and be loved, know peace and joy.
- The Throat Chakra's right is to express your truth, strengthen your willpower, have clear communication, be creative in your expression and live in integrity.
- The Brow Chakra's right is to think clearly, cultivate wisdom, knowledge and discernment, develop intuition and imagination.
- The Crown Chakra's right is to know beauty, serenity and your indelible connection to God.

By affirming your rights you strengthen your energy centers. These are archetypal ideas we can use as models for our inner development. They remind us who we are and what our inner work strives to accomplish.

...gels and
...ot Chakra

T he Root Chakra controls our physical life. This center anchors our life force in the physical plane. It insures our survival and the quality of the life we live. It sits at the base of the spine and is the first chakra to open and the last to heal. It contains all accumulated beliefs of family, school and religion, from generations about how we see and experience life.

If we had an ancestor who feared life and was highly ritualistic, appeasing the gods with sacrifice, we might find we re-enact the same drama around our fear of life. If we had ancestors who were angry and cruel to others in their greed for more possessions we might find this energy harbors itself within us. All these old familial patterns exist within us.

We hope to make them conscious so they don't wind up running our life. We cleanse the energy of the Root Chakra by examining the validity of our beliefs. We ask if they hold up as truthful ways of living our life now.

Contained within the Root Chakra are the qualities that help define the chakra's function. These qualities are: organization, administration, security, stability, and the ability to manifest our dreams into reality. This chakra resonates with the rhythms and cycles of life. Its music is rhythmic drum music that mirrors the primal rhythms of the heart and the breath.

The Root Chakra focuses on all we need for our physical survival. It teaches us to thrive where we are rooted. It is our foundation in life. How we handle change, experience moves, have a sense of haste or patience all reflect how the Root Chakra is functioning on our behalf. We are deeply dependent on the fiber and strength of this center to support us in life.

The Root Chakra thrives on constancy and functions well with stability. It enjoys the steady, plodding, daily activities that keep us rhythmic and regulated. It does best with routine and regular cycles. Its viability is dependent on our ability to adapt to change in all situations.

The Root Chakra has more unconsciousness patterns and beliefs within it than any other chakra. These become activated when our survival is threatened. It can become dysfunctional when we sustain a shock to our system. Whenever we face a threat or unknown danger the Root Chakra can become paralyzed and frozen. This can show up as problems with the pelvis, rectum, hips, legs and feet which channel the energy of this chakra.

It requires detachment to look at the attitudes we hold within our Root Chakra. Each step we take to define our right to our own life helps recalibrate its vibrations and strengthens its bond between our spirit and the earth.

When the Root Chakra is healthy it expands and supports life more fully. We feel we can take on more responsibilities, be more creative, and more playful. A healthy Root Chakra is flexible and, at the same time, enjoys the daily rhythms of life. When it is stable it allows for us to be more patient to see our good unfold. It is less volatile and reactive to how other people act, without taking offence at what they say and do. It has a natural buffer which permits us to accept life as it is. A healthy Root Chakra loves order, rhythm, security and stability.

Working with the angels and the Archangel Michael, who rules this chakra, helps us to anchor the life force fully within this center. Doing regular meditation, saying affirmations, and affirmative prayer are tools that help us skillfully become rooted in our life. It helps us manage change and adapt to new circumstances.

The angels of the Root Chakra help smooth the way for us to make wise choices for our life. Angels ease our transitions and life changes and help us settle in our skin as we adapt to new circumstances and environments. They help us keep our spiritual connections when the winds of change blow in our lives.

The qualities that fortify and stabilize the Root Chakra are:

Patience

Patience is indicative of a strong and healthy Root Chakra. If we are restless, constantly moving from place to place, job to job, relationship to relationship, the Root Chakra is both weak and undefined. It will not have strong boundaries that can hold the life force. This will create restlessness and a constant desire for change. We want to create a Root Chakra that is as strong as the concrete foundations of a house and can hold our life in place.

Patience is the defining quality of the Root Chakra. It allows us to firmly and fully "root" ourselves into life. Without a strong anchor the irregularities and mishaps of life will buffet us about and wreak havoc in our lives. Our spirit will not survive well with constant change and we will be like a feather in the wind. We can only be truly creative and happy when we are rooted in our own life.

Security

This quality regulates us and gives us a sense of well-being. It allows us to let down our guard, relax and recharge our energy. Security releases us from constantly being frightened and worried about our survival. Ultimately, it helps us create reserves of energy for getting through the challenging times.

We need to experience security in order to feel protected. Security lets us thrive, and in doing so we come to know the truth and beauty of our spirit. Security helps us keep our minds turned to the good. Security lets us define healthy boundaries and provide a margin for comfort, ease and assurance.

Stability

Stability keeps us steady through change. It implies being balanced, and having the ability to be flexible and to move with the times. It stops us becoming reactive or feeling threatened.

Stability allows us to focus on our inner world. It supports our awareness and gives us clear perceptions of the world around us. When we are stable we know what is best for us, and how to re-adjust ourselves to stay steady and constant. Stability helps us to trust in life.

Structure

Structure permits us to create rhythm and routines which define our daily activity. Structure supports us in maintaining a foundation that will hold our gifts and talents so they can develop. Structure gives strength and purpose to our efforts. Structure is power.

Building a structure to your day, week, month or year creates a rhythm that supports you in creating and maintaining the life you want. You can be flexible within it and deviate from it but you know your structure holds you steady. There is true power in a structure that includes your physical need for rest, sleep, nutrition, exercise, work and spirituality.

Manifestation

When we claim our good spiritually we need it to manifest in the material world around us. We may not have any idea how or when that will happen but we know it will unfold as we keep claiming that good.

As we claim our good we can see it manifest as greater health, more abundant prosperity, truly loving and wholesome relationships and successful projects. Manifestation is the external expression of God and the angels working in our lives.

Administration

This is the ability to organize and administer our lives so we have a sense of control of the external factors that influence us. It suggests order in how we use our time, energy and resources for our good. People who live in chaos and waste their vital life energy are neither grounded nor have functional Root Chakras.

We want to eliminate waste and dissipation because they interfere with the flow of life. People who have given up on their dreams have difficulties manifesting what they need for their survival. They often fall into despair. People who administer their lives carefully and realistically have a strong, healthy Root Chakra and keep chaos at bay. We want to remember that health is an organizing principle in which all systems are self-regulating and we experience abundant vitality and joy in being alive.

The Angels and the Root Chakra

The angels who govern the workings of our Root Chakra strengthen it through stability and constancy. They know that when we are rooted within ourselves, we have the possibility to be flexible in our thinking and open to new possibilities. They encourage us to adapt to change in order to remain healthy and in the flow of life.

A strong and healthy Root Chakra anchors us in the here and now. Angels can help us accommodate uncertainty when we are grounded in the everyday routines of life. They know we have the resilience to meet new challenges with patience and persistence.

Angels work to keep us stable and steady in the flow of life. Whenever a change threatens your inner stability, call on your angelic guides. They will help you connect to your roots and ground yourself in reality. With their help life falls back into its everyday routines and rhythms.

The Root Chakra is ruled by the angels, who are the first distinct category in the Heaven of Form. They are governed by the Archangel Michael, God's great emissary to humanity who brings justice to the souls of the dead. He is known as the General of the Heavenly Armies and fights for the good, the just and the true.

We cannot fail to find our feet on the ground, accepting reality squarely as it is when we call Michael to our side.

Developing a healthy Root Chakra requires cultivating patience, perseverance and discipline. These qualities keep us moving forward, dealing with contingencies and change. They ground our spirit in life. Michael and the angels work to instill these qualities that have served soldiers and warriors since humanity became an organized social structure.

Michael and the angels help us to stay the course of life. They encourage us to work hard, bring order out of chaos and move in the direction of our highest good. Prayer, meditation and affirmation support us through change because they anchor our spirit and keep us flexible and open. We can call on our angels to please help us when life feels precarious and we are uncertain as to our path.

The angels help us quiet our mind and open our heart in meditation and prayer. They want us spiritually open to receive our best. They inform us that love is possible, and joy is within our grasp. They do not want us falling into despair or fear, which can drain away life force and create illness and suffering. They teach us to ask for what we need and trust that what we want will come to us. They help us emerge victorious from the challenges of life.

Meditation on the Root Chakra

Meditating on the Root Chakra strengthens it. It fortifies our spirit's connection to the physical body and the earth plane. It helps heal feelings of disconnection, separation or loss. When we experience being uprooted, or anything which disrupts our daily rhythms, evokes fear or despair, meditation is the best tool to bring us back to center.

This meditation helps the angels create the inner forces we need to anchor our spirit solidly in physical reality. They insure that we are focused and organized and can accomplish our daily tasks.

We can invoke our angels through affirmations, positive prayer and meditation. When we think positive thoughts that focus on stability, wholeness and assurance they put these qualities into place within the platform of the Root Chakra. When we affirm that all is well then our experience is that. Meditation draws angels into our field to heal our wounds. They recalibrate the vibration of our chakras so they are resonant with cosmic forces that bring healing and harmony to us. They help release stagnant and congested energy that holds us back from our joy.

Whenever you experience a thought or belief that is punishing, unkind or cruel, especially at the expense of your well-being or confidence, take a deep breath into your Root Chakra and affirm your worth.

We live in a world full of negativity and it is so easy to see our inadequacies and failures. We expect so much of ourselves and it is all too easy to fall into negative thinking. Please reframe your thoughts to ones that are loving and worthy of your greatest good. This is how we develop compassion and love for ourselves. This is what angels do and why they accept and love us as we are.

Through inner work we open the channel to receive love when we affirm our lives and claim our highest good. The angels' gentleness and kindness help you to learn to reframe your beliefs about unworthiness. Angels always include you in their love for you. Include yourself as well.

MEDITATION

Begin this meditation by sitting in a comfortable position. Relax. Take several deep breaths and release any tension you feel.

As you sit quietly, focusing your awareness on your breath, begin to look inward. Release your jaw, allow your eyes to sink back into your head and literally blow the air out of your chest.

Continue to breathe in and breathe out, releasing any negative, limiting thoughts that suggest you are not good enough to be loved or deserve to have what you want in life. You know the litany of your own negativity better than anyone. Be willing to release it. Say goodbye to despair, fear and doubt.

Affirm your right to have the life you want. Know you are worthy of love, kindness and having your dreams come true. Each inhalation draws in the love of God; exhalation releases your fears, thoughts of unhappiness or worries. Angels will carry away your negativity and fill you with affirmative, positive energy that says "YES" to life.

Now tell yourself, "All is well." Repeat it as many times as it takes to know the truth of this statement. Affirm your right to your life. Affirm your right to enjoy happiness, feel fulfilled and experience prosperity and abundance in your life. Offer gratitude to your angels for their guidance and to God for the gift of life.

Gratitude heals dysfunction in all the chakras. It opens a field for grace to enter your being and carry you forward. It eases your way through challenges and difficulties.

Give thanks for all that you are, all that you have, all that you do. It is all a blessing. As you complete this meditation know you are deeply, deeply held by the angels of your life who deeply love you and adore you.

PRAYER FOR A HEALTHY AND STRONG ROOT CHAKRA

Beloved God, dearest Archangel Michael and my blessed Angels, please hear my prayer for stability, constancy and grounding. Please keep me safe in life and carry me forward. Help me release all negativity of Victimhood and Martyrdom that limits me from the joy of life. Help me know my direction, teach me to follow my heart to love and be joyful. Anchor my sense of self-worth strongly within me so I know I am always worthy of my own love. Give me courage to persevere at my tasks and to find strength and trust in the goodness of life.

AFFIRMATION

I am grounded in the truth, beauty and power of my being. I claim my right to my life NOW.

RIGHT

I claim my right to my own life.

The Domain of Archangel Michael

The Root Chakra is our energetic rock in life as is the Archangel Michael. He helps hold our spirit and encourages us to root ourselves into the physical world we call "reality." He connects us to the earth, and helps us survive. He helps build a strong and developed Root Chakra that allows us to fully engage in the world, meeting our needs. Michael helps us develop the skills and talents we need that will support us, and benefit our communities and the world.

Michael asks that we be organized, find a simple, rhythmic, orderly routine in our everyday life. He encourages us to create constancy, dependability and trust in order to thrive. He is the spiritual force that helps us create a healthy foundation that gives stability and strength.

Michael governs our ability to survive. He influences our physical health, as well as our mental and emotional attitudes about life. He helps us affirm life through creating the power of rhythm in our days, weeks, months and years.

The Root Chakra is the portal through which our good manifests and it is the great Archangel Michael whose power and strength ground that good and make it real in our lives.

Each quality of the Root Chakra has its own angel that enhances that good. If you feel insufficient in any of these qualities meditate and pray to that angel. Ask for what you need to create harmony and balance so that you experience feeling anchored in life.

The Archangel Michael's name means "In the likeness of God." Traditionally he is known as Commander-in-Chief of the Heavenly Armies. He fights against evil and chaos. He challenges slavery with impunity. He helps us stand in our strength and live with integrity.

Archangel Michael is patron saint of the Catholic church, and head of the state of Israel. He has eternally defended the underdog and champions the good. He defends our right to live our own life. He helps us live as free beings, capable of making good choices.

Michael is guardian to those who work in the public sector and for the general welfare of mankind. He is patron saint to fire-fighters, policemen and women. He protects members of the armed forces and all who keep the high watch for the good of humanity.

Michael intervenes on our behalf when we need help with life and when we seek protection. Invoke his name when you are frightened, unsure, or lost. He will help you fight for your life. Calling him into our life always puts us on higher ground. Remember him as a great source of power and strength.

Michael will keep you from harm's way. He will guide you through the unknown and act as guide and protector to you and your dear ones. He will keep you steady through change, because he represents God's truth, integrity, and strength.

He offers humanity the highest level of protection so we can live in safety and love. With Michael at our side we know, in our heart of hearts, that we are safe. We call on him to preserve our well-being and watch over those we love. His domain is earth and his reign brings humanity God's love and power.

MEDITATION ON THE ARCHANGEL MICHAEL
AND THE ROOT CHAKRA

Sit quietly. Relax. Breathe into your Root Chakra. Scan your body for areas of tension you may be holding. Breathe into any place that is tight, congested or sore.

Feel the strong and competent arms of the Archangel Michael holding your Root Chakra steady and firmly in place. Michael will not let you fall or fail in life. He watches your back and protects you against all harm. In his arms you are always steady, safe and stable.

You can invoke Archangel Michael at any time. Feel his strength and grace filling your body and the spirit of him guiding you to higher ground. You may not know the path but you will know you are safe and protected as you travel the journey of life.

You will feel strength in your spine, in the core of your belly, down your legs and in your feet. This comes from calling Michael to you. Visualize the strength and power of Michael working in you. This is God's might that he channels on behalf of all humanity.

Feel him beside you; standing tall and secure. He is like a great rock that shields you and protects you. He supports you standing upright, living in truth and in your integrity. He is one of the greatest spiritual resources we have for our well-being and protection.

PRAYER TO MICHAEL

Beloved Michael, thank you for loving and
protecting me through all the changes of my life.
Thank you for keeping me steady, stable and true to
my inner knowledge that life is good and I am safe.
I know you are always by my side and hold me up.
Please stand with me now and help me overcome

my fears and doubts. I long for happiness, and to
find fulfillment in my life. I long for peace and
to feel love fill my life. Thank you for the courage
to stand tall and walk with me. I am so grateful for
your steadfast strength that holds me upright.

AFFIRMATION

I stand in my truth and live from my integrity.

Angels of the Root Chakra

The Angel of the Earth

The Angel of the Earth governs our planet's spiritual evolution. She
offers humanity a path to healing that sustains and protects our
planet. Just as an individual experiences personal growth and transformation, so the earth evolves and develops. She matures as a spiritual force in the universe and becomes conscious, just as we do.

The earth's spiritual awakening depends on our ability to
expand our consciousness and transform what imperils and
threatens her existence. All life exists in the Divine Presence and
the earth is a living being.

We are all connected to the great universal life force we know
as God. We live it, breathe it and share it together. There is no
separation in this realm of existence.

The Angel of the Earth transforms the atrocious acts of abuse,
violence and destruction perpetrated against her. She is constantly
renewing earth's forces and healing her spirit. She regards the
earth as a sacred vessel that supports life.

113

MEDITATION

Sit comfortably. Relax and breathe deeply. Scan your body for areas of tension. Release these areas through your breath. Visualize the earth as if you were looking at her from far space. See the globe held in the arms of this great Angel of the Earth.

She is enormous and her vast wings expand far out into space. She supports our planet. She breathes deeply into the core of the earth to keep it alive and her fires burning brightly. She cleanses the seas and purifies the air. Bless earth so she can sustain us. She imbues our planet with love, and offers us the intelligent solutions needed for our survival.

PRAYER TO THE ANGEL OF THE EARTH

Beloved Angel of the Earth, thank you for holding the life of our planet close to your heart and keeping her forces renewed. Protect her and help her. Please awaken our consciousness to ways we can offer her healing. We petition you to bring healing to us all.

AFFIRMATION

I bless the earth with love. I vow to be a steward to protect her spirit.

The Guardian Angels

Our guardian angels protect and guide us. They connect all individual souls to the universal life force we call God. They guide us through eternity, and stay with us over lifetimes. They support our soul's evolution to experience higher levels of love and greater truths in each incarnation. They help us develop an awakened consciousness through all our experiences.

Our guardians work within this expanded consciousness to bring greater love and deeper spirituality to us. They ask that we affirm our worth and always honor our choices for love. They empower us to be co-creators of our life, always claiming our good and acknowledging God as Source.

Our guardians carry us forward through all conditions, experiences and situations. They support our choices for empowerment and, ultimately, for healing. They stand by us always as the great, guiding spiritual forces that know us thoroughly. They strive to awaken us to the truth of ourselves. They are our friends and pray we realize our worth. They stand alongside us through all our challenges. They never abandon us, even when we make less than wholesome choices.

It is an act of love and gratitude to say thank you for all they have done for us. They delight in our joy and happiness and they love being thanked. They want us to always choose our highest good and greatest joy.

MEDITATION

Sit comfortably. Relax and breathe deeply. Release tension with each exhalation. With each inhalation draw in the love and protection of your guardian angel. It is there waiting for you to feel that warmth and protection it provides for you.

Your guardian angel is right next to you, right now. They never exit the premises or go out for lunch. You can sense them in your field if you are very still. Their joy is to nourish your soul and soothe your spirit. Each breath you take brings you closer to the Divine Presence. They strengthen you and love you.

Feel yourself carried in the arms of love by your guardian angel. As you begin to trust its presence ask for guidance. This is a way in which your guardian angel can help you and serve your happiness and wholeness.

PRAYER TO YOUR GUARDIAN ANGEL

Beloved guardian angel, who has known me through lifetimes, I thank you for your love, protection and guidance. I appreciate your vigilance and constancy in watching over my soul. You have given me encouragement when life seemed unmanageable, kudos when I achieved a merit and you have held me through all the fears, doubts and losses of my life. Thank you for showing me the way home to my spirit and to know God as the living force within me. I know how deeply you love me. Show me how to deepen my trust in life and surrender to a higher good. Thank you.

I affirm that I am loved and guided through eternity by
my guardian angel. I know I am blessed.

The Angel of Community

The Angel of Community offers us inclusion into the love and
warmth of community. It allows us to express our hopes and
dreams and to share them with others. Community is how we
unite our spirits for the common good.

This angel brings God's love to all groups and communities striving to know love, healing and wholeness for the world. It invites
all members of community to collaborate for the highest good.

Community provides each individual with a unique opportunity to be of value. Community says each person has something
special to offer. It encourages the sharing of new ideas and shines
light on all who participate in community. Community replaces
the old concept of tribe and division; community is oneness.

MEDITATION

Sit comfortably. Relax and breathe deeply. Scan your
body for areas of tension. Breathe deeply into those
areas. Feel your sense of oneness with life. Ask yourself
where and who is your community? Who are the people
you resonate with? Where are the people who share your
ideas and who support you in being and doing your best?
Think of the greater human community of which you are
a part.

Envision happiness, fulfillment and oneness for all people in your community. Be blessed as you consciously create a sense of oneness with them. We are one people, one planet and part of an expanding network of consciousness capable of doing great good.

PRAYER TO THE ANGEL OF COMMUNITY

Beloved Angel of Community, please bless all communities that strive for good and especially those that honor spirit. Let the spirit shine in all places where people come together for a greater good. Help them unite and work together. Bless them for their individual efforts and collective manifestations on behalf of the whole.

AFFIRMATION

I affirm that I am a part of the family of man.
I bless all communities that honor the spirit
of oneness.

CHAPTER 6

The Archangels and the Sacral Chakra

The archangels represent the second tier within the Heaven of Form. They bring us the power of light by which we "see" the spiritual truths. This light embodies strength, healing and love. It is incorporated in our field as the light that shines from within us.

The archangels are said to be the bearers of sunlight to earth. They created light by which we live in the physical world and see in the spiritual realm. The archangels have a deep, abiding bond to the Christ, who is also the bearer of light. There are said to be twelve archangels in number and they represent the twelve aspects of the Christ.

The archangels govern the Sacral Chakra, located in the abdomen, above the Root Chakra. This center focuses on abundance, health, unconditional love, pleasure and ease. Archangels help us develop these qualities within ourselves. The healing of this chakra and the development of these qualities is an essential aspect of our spirituality.

The archangels inform the Sacral Chakra and implant a balance between a good work ethic and giving permission for delight and pleasure. This energy center contracts in pain and opens with pleasure. It requires a balance of forces to maintain its health.

Archangels awaken our senses and influence our ability to control our appetite. They teach us to seek the balance between what is enough and what is sufficient to meet our needs. They stimulate a consciousness of greed and sufficiency so we can gauge when we have crossed the line of too much.

They aim to create well-being and balance within each individual. They help the "gut" know satiety, and they teach the mind that what we have and do is enough.

Knowing what is sufficient is the key to health and the logo for the archangels who work in this chakra. Sufficiency can be anything from the amount of food we eat to the amount of exercise we do. It can refer to how much money we need or how much rest and relaxation we allow ourselves. Balance and fair measure are keynotes of the Sacral Chakra.

This is the center of physical health and the immune system. It controls physical movement as well as elegance. It is a primary center of activity for athletes, singers and dancers. When we honor the needs of the Sacral Chakra we create health, well-being and balance in this center.

The Sacral Chakra becomes fully functional between the ages of seven and fourteen years old. This chakra stimulates hormonal flow which targets reproduction, sexuality, and physical well-being. It holds the reserves of physical energy we will need to see us through crisis, illness and depletion.

The energy in this chakra is dependent on how we feel and express our emotions. The Sacral Chakra energy expands with self-acceptance and love and contracts with self-loathing. We feel good when we take care of ourselves and punished when we don't.

Its function depends on wholesome and healthy ideas about who we are and what we feel we deserve. It is a center capable of holding our resilience, strength, beauty, and pleasure. This is operational at any age. We can keep it vital and alive till we die by loving ourselves and honoring our bodies' need for pleasure.

If we do not feel we are good enough for what we say we want we will punish our bodies trying to make them better. We will submit to procedures that bruise, hurt and paralyze the body's ability to regenerate itself. Demanding a perfect body in order to be loved is one of the great delusions of our age. When we abuse our bodies they become unable to be receptors for pleasure and joy.

Learn to love the body, and honor its needs for what will support its durability and delight for years. Cultivating healthy attitudes that enhance this chakra keep us vital for years. We can build this chakra at any age. And we can heal our dysfunctional attitudes about sexuality, prosperity, health and pleasure at any time in life by allowing the archangels to fill our being with light.

The life issues and challenges of the Sacral Chakra encompass most of humanity's desires and longings. It is the most dysfunctional chakra in the human energy system, corrupted by greed and repeated abuse. A balanced outlook about sexuality and money, self-acceptance, and our right to pleasure keeps this chakra bountiful and fluid as a person matures.

The Sacral Chakra is dysfunctional because of greed and temptation. In western culture, with its demands for easy consumption and possessions, our natural life energy has become weakened and dissipated. If there is no spiritual dimension in a person's life then energy will eventually stagnate and congest in this center. This can lead to health problems.

It takes both will and intelligence to honor the needs of this chakra. Finding healthy guidelines that map out what is enough helps us create good boundaries. The archangels neither judge, punish, nor condemn what we do, at any age. They do, however, encourage us to live a healthy life that supports the spirit. They want us to enjoy the fruits of life from experiencing our worth. They encourage us to find joy, pleasure and prosperity without guilt, shame or humiliation.

Physical movement supports and strengthens the Sacral Chakra. Dance, sports and different forms of physical activity keep the flow of vitality moving in this chakra. Choosing the right measure of physical activity, without becoming compulsive or obsessive, allows the spirit to be free.

Working closely with the angelic forces, through prayer, meditation, and reflective practice establishes a spiritual presence in this center. Remember the entire western world's second chakra is distorted and damaged. It needs spiritual forces to correct this imbalance. It takes a mature consciousness to realize that gentleness, tenderness and love can heal this center.

The archetypal qualities of the Sacral Chakra have to do with pleasure and love.

Health

Health is vitality and resilience, and comes from our core animal energy. Health means we have regenerative ability and can create reserves of energy for times of challenge. We want enough health to have energy for our work and our pleasure.

Being healthy requires a willingness to move and live the life of the body. Exercise stimulates the circulation, removes toxicity and nourishes the cells. Eating healthy food supplies the body with nourishment. Learning what supports a healthy Sacral

Chakra, how much and how little, gives us power over our health.

Learning to love the body, just exactly as it is, is the gift of a healthy and loving mind. Building in pleasure, giving the body time for rest and regeneration is essential for a good, long life.

Unconditional Love

Our levels of unconditional love bring healing to everything we do. Unconditional love is behind every experience we have. Our ability to love ourselves, forgive the past and honor our needs defines us. It is through unconditional love for ourselves that we bring the forces of healing into our lives.

It implies we love ourselves without reserve or doubt. How we honor our needs, feel our feelings and express our truth is a measure of how well we love ourselves. People who do not love themselves are condemning, harsh and punishing. How they treat themselves is how they will treat others.

When we love ourselves unconditionally we accept who we are. We accept our imperfections, limitations and uncertainty. We stop the inner conflict and release fear that we are not good enough. We stop eating away at our self-worth and find the kind, tender way of embracing our wounds.

Love and forgiveness release the grip of negativity that we allow to hold power over us. Unconditional love puts an end to sacrifice and a need to prove our worth. It frees us to live our lives.

Pleasure and Ease

Ease and pleasure fuel our well-being. They provide joy and are essential components for a healthy, physical life. They are the ways we relax, let down our hair and have fun. They are not an end in themselves but rewards for hard work and responsibility.

Maturity requires balance between being able to work hard and play well. Maturity also accepts the complexity of both hardship and ease, frivolity and gravity. It strives for balance whenever possible.

Real ease involves doing what you like, when you like. People who work and toil too hard are martyrs. They dry up and they lose their edge. People who indulge themselves too much, without responsibilities, are spoiled and narcissistic. Finding the middle ground requires the balance of self-love and discipline.

Abundance and Prosperity

Prosperity and abundance reflect a belief in our innate worth to be loved, blessed and fully supported by God. They are a central theme of the Sacral Chakra.

Spiritual teaching says money and love come from God. Allowing prosperity to come into your life reflects a belief that you are worthy of receiving your good. You acknowledge it as your right when you claim it for yourself.

God and His angels provide for us freely. It is ours to know that we are worthy of what we say we want in our lives. Trusting that it is ours takes great faith.

Believe God wants you to be happy and enjoy the fruits of His garden. Envision a wealth of goodness flowing to you. Be open to receiving your highest good and greatest joy and it will heal and strengthen your Sacral Chakra. Abundance reflects your right to pleasure. Call it to you now.

MEDITATION ON THE SACRAL CHAKRA

Sit comfortably. Relax. Take several deep breaths. Scan your body for areas of tension. Release the tension by breathing into those areas. As you relax feel the flow of energy in your body.

Fill the tense places in your body with pink light. It will ease and dissipate the tightness with each exhalation. Green and pink, blue and violet are the colors that ease pain and release tension. Red, orange and yellow fill areas that are cold, numb or lifeless. They energize your body.

Orange is a sensual and relaxing color because it contains the qualities of pleasure, warmth and ease. It invites you to let go, ease down and relax. Now, fill your entire abdomen with orange light and let it radiate out of your body. See it as your connection to the things that delight you and give you pleasure.

The four archangels of health, unconditional love, pleasure and abundance reside in this chakra. They strive to bring you the love, healing and pleasure you deserve. Begin to call the archangels into your awareness. They add light and warmth to your Sacral Chakra and fill your Sacral Chakra with energy that feels good and is comforting.

Ask the archangels to help you with problems in this area. They can help you find the solutions you need to your

125

problems. Ask the archangels to release tension, fear, stress or abuse from this center. As you relax and ease down into your body begin to feel at home in your self. Now forgive the past, release hurt, let go.

As you breathe into the Sacral Chakra, fill your pelvis with the warmth of your own love. Feel your lower back relax and ease down as you release pressure to perform, or be more than you are. Knowing you are enough just exactly as you are is what heals this center. Affirm that you are a child of God; worthy of love, prosperity, good health and happiness. It is yours when you claim it.

PRAYER FOR THE SACRAL CHAKRA

Beloved archangels who govern the Sacral Chakra, please support me in letting go of old thoughts that haunt my mind with beliefs of unworthiness and self-loathing. Help me know my wholeness. Teach me to accept myself as I am. Help me create more balance, deeper acceptance, and abiding self-love. Teach me to love myself through all my faults, imperfections and limitations. In gratitude, I offer my love and thanks to you.

AFFIRMATION

I know and trust that who I am, what I have and all that I do are enough. I love and accept myself exactly as I am.

I claim my right to pleasure, health, prosperity
and well-being.

The Domain of Archangel Metatron

The archangels have a special relationship with light that brings
warmth and healing to this center. It needs strong and affirmative
forces like the archangels to keep this center functional. The
archangel who governs this chakra is known as Archangel Metatron.

He is thought to have been the Patriarch Enoch who lived in
biblical times. He was known for being a righteous man who did
good. He had a deep sense of justice and knew the fair measure of
all things.

It is said the angels loved him so much they took him into the
heavenly realms and made him an archangel to help heal humanity.
He reminds us to seek balance in all we do and to know that who
we are and what we do are always enough.

Knowing the fair measure of all things helps us stay centered in
our being. This applies to our resources of time, money and energy.
Knowing the fair measure of all things helps us form healthy boundaries. This conserves our energy and keeps us joyful and happy.

Archangel Metatron is a guiding force for our age, where excess
is the norm and boundaries are nearly non-existent. Our culture is
out of balance; few people truly know what is enough, and, in that
misunderstanding, they are always striving for more.

Archangel Metatron helps overcome addictions and obsessions,
which are another form of not being enough. He helps us find
balance and healing in this center. He needs our prayers to bring us
all protection and guidance.

MEDITATION

Sit comfortably. Relax. Take several deep breaths. Feel at ease sitting and focusing on your breath. There is nothing else you need do. Reflect on what feels good to you. Do you know when you have enough? Are you stretched, trying to do too much, or are you bored with not enough to do? Where is your balance?

Reflect on the Archangel Metatron and on your Sacral Chakra. How can he help you know that all that you are and all that you do are enough? Can you create an internal measure that lets you feel you are enough?

Archangel Metatron is fully aware of our human frailty. He knows we have a need to constantly prove our worth. He knows we overdo things and that sometimes we don't do enough. He does not judge or punish. He hopes we get the fair measure of our value so we can calibrate our energy better.

As you sit in silence and reflect on your "enough-ness" have a sense that who you are, what you have and what you do are truly enough. Find peace in this truth and let it still your nerves and release tension.

PRAYER

Beloved Metatron, please guide me in meeting my body's need for rest and recreation. Help me know when to stop overdoing, when to slow down and let life be.

Help me create healthy boundaries that support me and help me experience my joy. Show me that I do not have to toil to receive God's bounty. It can come to me because of who I am. Help me open myself to receiving this good. Thank you.

I open myself to receiving the fair measure of my good.

Archangels of the Sacral Chakra

The Archangel Michael

Although Michael is the archangel who governs the Root Chakra, he also works within the field of the Sacral Chakra. He stops us from falling into victimhood, and becoming the underdog. He encourages us to see life through responsible eyes that know balance.

Michael keeps us connected to our earthly roots. He supports the Sacral Chakra by keeping us safe and honoring our needs for pleasure and fun. He asks us to keep life simple, full of love, humor and kindness.

He encourages us to create healthy boundaries so we can manage our lives appropriately, and deal with the complexity of modern life. Michael strives to create healthy people who have abundant reserves of energy.

Sit quietly. Relax. Connect with your breath. Scan your body for areas of tension. Release any tension through your breath.

As you settle into yourself reflect on your right to pleasure and ease. Feel your belly expand in pleasure and delight. Can you identify what gives you pleasure?

Your right to pleasure belongs to you. You can choose to follow your pleasure when you need time off and a rest. Archangel Michael guards the portals of your life. He keeps you safe so that you can be happy and enjoy yourself.

PRAYER

Beloved Michael, thank you for your willingness to stand by me and help me find my happiness and seek my pleasure. Thank you for your protection and guidance. Please keep me safe, healthy, and resilient so that I can have fun and enjoy myself. Help me do the best I am able to do and also to respect my need for pleasure and fun. Help me enjoy my life.

AFFIRMATION

I am grateful for pleasure and fun. They bring joy and a deeper sense of myself.

The Archangel Gabriel

Archangel Gabriel's name means "Word of God." He is the one who helps us express our truth. He teaches us to speak up, and ask for what we want and need. When we feel constricted he guides us to find our joy.

His relationship to the Sacral Chakra is defined through our ability to communicate our needs, desires and wants. He helps us speak up for what we long for and teaches us to tell the truth to ourselves about what will make us happy. He assists us in making the choice for what and who will make us happy.

As we develop confidence in our ability to express our selves we share our feelings with ease and grace. We express our thoughts and opinions to those who are interested in our ideas and we find people who validate our truth.

There is a strong link between the Sacral Chakra with its desires and longings and the Throat Chakra with its capacity for self-expression. The link between archangels Gabriel and Metatron is the link between expression and desire. We don't need to be dramatic, manipulative or false in asking for what we want. We simply need to know what will make us feel good.

MEDITATION

Begin this meditation by sitting quietly. Relax. Take several deep breaths. As you settle into yourself scan your body for areas of tension. Release this tension with your breath.

Begin this meditation by asking yourself the question: what will give me pleasure now? The more you are aware of your feelings and what you desire the easier it is to tell yourself the truth.

Knowing what you feel increases your ability to express your truth. Your emotions may feel awkward and confusing at first; or you may lack a sense of safety in expressing them. As you develop the skill of differentiating what you feel it becomes easier to express your truth. With practice you develop a way of sharing your feelings with others.

PRAYER

Beloved Archangel Gabriel, help me feel my feelings and express my truth. Help me feel safe sharing the deepest parts of me. Thank you for an awareness of my feelings and the safety to tell myself the truth about what I hope and long for in life. Help me stay open and loving to the truth of myself.

AFFIRMATION

I honor my feelings and express my truth to the best of my ability.

The Archangel Uriel

The Archangel Uriel brings the light of our inner sun into resonance with the outer world. He represents the light of God. He rules the Solar Plexus which is located above the Sacral Chakra, just over the stomach area. Its central theme is self-worth and empowerment. This archangel supports the healing of the Sacral Chakra, just as the Archangel Michael does. It radiates our inner light into this chakra to heal what has been darkened by a lack of self-love.

When we know we are worthy of love, kindness and respect we avoid destructive behavior that puts us at risk. Preserving our self-respect allows all our organs to receive optimal energy. When, for any reason, we give ourselves away too easily we lose that energetic connection to the Sacral Chakra. Then we need to re-work this center, feeding it with love, care and self-love.

This archangel stimulates the Solar Plexus to expand our sense of self-worth, self-confidence and personal power to incorporate the Sacral center. Archangel Uriel helps us live our worthiness and find our freedom from abusive situations which diminish our value.

Archangel Uriel heals any loss of self-respect. He helps us find empowerment in our own value so we can shine our light on to the world and claim our good. He represents the inner values of Selfhood which are rooted in self-love, self-respect and self-expression. This is what fortifies the Sacral Chakra.

MEDITATION

Sit quietly. Relax. Breathe gently. Pay attention to your inhalation and exhalation. Scan your body for areas of tension. Breathe into any place that may be tense.

As you experience your body hold the thought that you are a valuable human being, worthy of love, and open to kindness. You are a light in the world and you deserve affection and love.

The Archangel Uriel supports you knowing your value. He wants you to learn to honor your needs and to treat yourself respectfully. Allow yourself to love your body, accept your emotions and pay attention to your thoughts.

You do not need to be perfect in order to accept yourself. There is nothing you have to achieve to have self-respect or value. You are worthy because you exist. Self-love paves the way for goodness to come to you. The angels always affirm you and when you honor yourself you feel this goodness in your life.

PRAYER

Beloved Uriel, help me honor my needs and stay open to healing the wounds of my past. I am grateful for the joy and ease that self-love affords me. I feel well when I move easily, and look after myself. I am better able to experience the joys of life. I know that I am more than a physical body, and I honor the temple of my spirit. Please help me take care of myself so I can know my worth and accept the truth of me as a child of God.

AFFIRMATION

I honor myself as a child of God and a gift to the world. I take care of myself, and treat myself respectfully.

The Archangel Raphael

The Archangel Raphael brings God's healing love to humanity. He governs the Heart Chakra forces that let love flow through us. He knows us as whole, complete and worthy of receiving that love. He heals the wounds of pain, loss and separation with love.

In biblical texts he was portrayed carrying a large book listing all the plants used for healing. He is God's healer and for generations doctors and healers have turned to him asking for God's grace to heal the sick. He guides us to health, relieves pain and stops our suffering.

Archangel Raphael recognizes the perfection of the spirit in each individual. He brings us awareness of our Divine nature, which is love. He assures us we are whole. He helps us accept God's love with humility and peace.

Archangel Raphael opens our hearts and minds to our true goodness and the light that we are. He softens our hearts through the power of love and eases those self-limiting beliefs that block us from receiving our good.

When we open our hearts we are grateful for love in all its many forms. We acknowledge the healing we have experienced. Archangel Raphael helps us open to love, soften our hearts and let in the good.

God works through us to be channels of His love. The power of the Archangel Raphael opens our Sacral Chakra to the love of God. He helps open our center to receive God's blessings for health, wholeness, pleasure and abundance. This is the center of balance where wisdom and maturity can preserve our life force.

MEDITATION

Sit quietly. Relax. Consciously release the cares of the external world with each exhalation. Allow love and peace to quietly and gently fill your spirit. Breathe into your Sacral Chakra and release tension, fear and any lack of confidence you feel about yourself.

Imagine God's healing love with every inhalation and

135

with each exhalation, releasing illness, suffering and tension. Release any mental ideas of separation that limit you from receiving God's love in your body through your breath. Let yourself be filled with love and feel healing happening as you let go.

Know deep in your heart you are worthy of healing. Allow light and goodness to fill you and carry you towards greater levels of self-acceptance.

PRAYER

Beloved Raphael, thank you for the healing love that fills my soul. I ask you to heal my Sacral Chakra, worn by fear that I wasn't enough. Please help me be strong, resilient, sensual and alive again and fill me up with vibrant health. Help me develop a trust in myself, find wisdom from my experiences and come to a still place of unconditional love. Help me forgive the hurts from the past and help me know I am worthy of love.

AFFIRMATION

I willingly release what is stagnant and old, cold and unfeeling, congested and blocked in my Sacral Chakra. I open myself to receiving joy in all ways that link me with pleasure, joy and delight to the Source.

CHAPTER 7

The Archai and the Solar Plexus Chakra

The Archai rule the Solar Plexus. They are also known as angel princes. They influence the four directions of the compass, and rule over nations and provinces. Each city, town, and village has its own angel prince.

The Archai govern continents and vast, uninhabited regions of the world. They help us locate ourselves in the world. They work individually and globally, instilling worth, pride of place and self-confidence. They honor locality, region and distinct cultures.

They affect our individual personalities by stimulating the Solar Plexus chakra. They help us build and connect to a deeper sense of the "I AM THAT I AM" principle. This is known as the Solar Logos, the definitive statement and universal expression of God that lives within us. It is the core spiritual truth of each person.

Spiritual consciousness is dependent on us accessing this principle. Once we have anchored and integrated this principal we interface with the world from a place of empowerment and compassion.

The Archai honor what is unique and special about us; they are the angels of personality. They help us develop our individual and unique personalities, our sense of humor and fun and whatever earmarks our individuality. They remind us we are unlike anyone else on earth and carry our own gifts and special qualities that make us special.

The Solar Plexus is where we define our personal identity. The Archai, as ancient tradition reveals, helped man stand upright and walk on two legs, beginning the long path towards individuation. It is also said that the Christ helped man become a strong individual through accepting the concept of the forgiveness of sins. Christ is seen to be the Solar Logos made flesh.

These powerful spiritual forces work within us to expand our self-worth, enhance our self-respect and honor the I AM within us. They work to develop a greater sense of self-esteem within us and help us claim freedom of choice. These are huge developments in the evolution of human consciousness, not to be taken lightly.

They empower us to express the choices that define us and to honor our personality as the individual manifestation of our light. What we like, desire, and choose are reflections of our individual choices. The Archai want us to be individuals, not imitations of others.

The Archai exist as radiant forms of light. Lightning and fire are the signs of their fantails. They work to strengthen and define our inner light and empower us to shine. They stimulate the Solar Plexus by shining their light on our light. They connect us to our true worth, which is our true value.

The Archai carry us through the emotional and spiritual initiations that make us strong, resilient and more conscious individuals. These experiences teach us who we are at a foundational level. No one can diminish this foundation because it is the rock of Self that illuminates our world.

The Archai empower us to stand upright, make wise decisions and to use our power with intelligence. "I AM THAT I AM" are sacred words that convey the power of the Divine Presence within us. These words resonate within the soul of each individual. The Archai implant them within the Solar Plexus believing they can be integrated into our waking consciousness.

The Solar Plexus is located below the sternum and over the stomach. This is the point where the body's largest nerve ganglions meet. It is very sensitive to external impressions and can become dysfunctional through stress, fear and confusion.

When this chakra is too open people pick up vibrations and impressions too easily from others. They may have difficulty differentiating what is them and what is another. This chakra also controls digestion and elimination in the body. It helps us digest new ideas as well as food. It is a focal point for healing the wounds of poor self-worth and low self-esteem. The Solar Plexus stimulates energy in the stomach, liver and gallbladder, pancreas and small and large intestines. These organs all connect with this chakra.

The chakra develops between the ages of 21 and 28. This is the time in which we define our self in life. It is also when we learn to negotiate with the world around us. In cultivating our personal identity we develop the Solar Plexus Chakra.

Here are some of the qualities of the Solar Plexus Chakra:

Self-Worth

This is the primary quality of the Solar Plexus. It is a measure of how much we love and value ourselves. The more we value ourselves the less dependent we are on the world to define us.

We create our own identity rather than the world giving us an identity.

Self-worth develops from infancy; it takes form in the ways in which we confront life's challenges. Our worth is innate to us; it comes from being human. Sometimes it takes many years to develop. All challenges strengthen the chakra and give it form and feeling.

Learning that we are always worthy of love, kindness and respect is a fundamental truth of the Solar Plexus. This truth releases us from having to prove ourselves to others. It makes us intolerant of abuse, or anything that diminishes our value.

When we connect to self and identify with our sacred nature we know we are worthy of whatever we claim for ourselves. We accept ourselves exactly as we are and we love ourselves. We are never too old, too fat, too ugly, too tired, or too poor. When we negate our worthiness we lose our power. We give it to others to define us.

Self-Respect

Self-respect defines the boundary of what is acceptable and what is not in our lives. It needs to inform our actions, and allow us to draw a line in the sand of what is acceptable to us and what is not. It protects our wholeness, our dignity and our value. It keeps what is noble shining brightly like gold. It prevents the spirit from being tarnished.

Self-respect lets us say no when boundaries are crossed. It affirms that we unconditionally love and respect ourselves, without amendment. Self-respect invites the good and keeps out the bad. Self-respect forms a natural boundary that filters out unkindness and bad behavior from others. It is a way that the angels protect our precious selfhood.

Self-Esteem

Self-esteem affirms the hard work and levels of accomplishment we have achieved in our life. It comes when we do our best and are proud of our efforts. It can mean doing well at games, being responsible for a family member, standing up for what we know is right. It is what we are most proud of, not what the world defines for us.

Self-esteem builds character. It defines the way in which we value our actions and efforts. These may be small and uneventful to others but have importance to us. It honors the light in us.

Self-Confidence

Self-confidence comes when we know we can do something well. It says we have moved beyond our fears and doubts to a level where we can manage our lives. To a certain degree, it implies we have both accomplishments and skills. Self-confidence tells us we can meet our challenges head on, without fear or cowardice.

When we have self-confidence we develop greater levels of personal power. Self-confidence allows our natural sense of worth to shine through. It develops our willingness to address the challenges we meet with a certainty that we can do our best.

Empowerment

Empowerment comes from knowing our strengths, living our truth and always choosing to be free and unrestricted in our personal expression. Developing personal power says to the world that we know how to be responsible for our actions and our choices. When we accept power we place ourselves in the stream of life, we know how to go with the flow, and do the dance of life with dexterity and grace.

Empowerment is not about what we do to others or what is done to us. It is the development of inner strength that says we know who we are, what we want and are willing to be responsible for claiming that good now for ourselves.

Personal power comes from becoming empowered. It comes from going within ourselves and affirming our lives, knowing we have a place in the universe and we do make a difference. Empowerment comes from harvesting out blame and anger. It asks us to develop a real sense of who we are and acknowledge the gifts we have which enable us to be a force for good in the world.

Freedom of Choice

Ultimately, all the qualities of the Sacral Chakra lead to freedom. Freedom is the acknowledgment of our worth, self-esteem, levels of confidence and empowerment. Freedom is totally about our ability to choose our good.

In freedom we choose the best of life for ourselves. We call in love, beauty, health, prosperity, unity, peace and joy to fulfill our lives. We claim our freedom to live a good life and we claim that for ourselves. As we mature we value freedom as one of the greatest gifts of life. Integrating it is how we claim our God-given gifts and talents and how we express our being in the world. Living in freedom takes choice to the highest level of personal expression.

The Archai and the Solar Plexus

The Archai applaud freedom of choice. They encourage us to become empowered and live freely. They ask us to always see the glass as half full rather than half empty. They help us turn around any belief that has us victimized. They ask us to own anything that is responsible for creating our life as a path to knowledge and power.

Freedom, one of the greatest gifts from the Divine, is governed by the Archai. It defines our actions, our attitudes and our levels of personal responsibility. If we do not experience freedom to choose our good, whatever comes to us will seem a random excuse from the universe. When we choose freely and consciously we are fully empowered, responsible and better able to enjoy our good.

The Archai support us through challenging initiations that empower us and strengthen our being. There is nothing that can diminish us if we take responsibility for it in our lives. We are free to love, forgive and heal.

The Archai keep us aware and conscious that we must honor our worth and choose love whenever possible if we want healing to go to the depths of our foundation. They hold the mirror of experience in front of us to reflect whether our choices serve us well or not.

They instill spiritual knowledge in our consciousness that encourages freedom and ask us to stop being slaves to external ideas, or situations and people that fail to recognize our worth and treat us with respect. They are the champions of freedom from oppression of all variety. They want us to be strong, capable warriors for truth and healing.

We can call on them in prayer, meditation, affirmation and reflective practice. We ask that they bring us strength and tenacity, the ability to remain stable and constant in our pursuit of the good. We ask their help in remembering our worth and we need them to help us make worthy choices for our good.

MEDITATION ON THE SOLAR PLEXUS

Sit comfortably. Relax and take several deep breaths. As you scan your body release tension by breathing deeply into that area. Feel your spine straighten as you release your jaw, relax your back, expand your shoulders. Feel your shoulders widen as your breath deepens and expands in your chest. Breathe into your Solar Plexus and say to yourself:

I am worthy of love, kindness and respect.

I know I am always worthy.

Know you are worthy of all you claim for yourself. Be respectful of your spirit's longing for love, kindness and understanding. Allow yourself to love who you are, what you have done with your life and all that you have survived to be here today. Call to you that which you know you want. Know you fully deserve it. This comes from the truth of your being and your right to claim your good.

Your worth, strength and power are loved and protected by the Archai. As you develop and strengthen these

144

qualities in yourself you will become a source of healing to the planet and to all those around you. You have the freedom to choose how and with whom you wish to share your light. Choose carefully. Trust that what you envision for your good is manifesting now.

PRAYER

Beloved Archai, help me to know the truth of my being and to experience my power and freedom. Help me grow into these qualities with wisdom and honesty. Help me develop a consciousness that can grow into love that can heal. Help me know I am worthy of all I say I want for myself. I ask to be released from the slavery to ideas that keep me a prisoner of guilt, shame and punishment. Help me forgive others as I release feelings of inadequacy, worthlessness and uselessness. Guide me to people who will help me honor the light within me. Help me be the person I know I can be.

AFFIRMATION

I know I am worthy of my own love and respect.
I gift myself with the truth of my light.

RIGHT

I claim my right to experience my worth
and know my value.

The Domain of Archangel Uriel

The Archangel Uriel rules the Solar Plexus Chakra. He helps us develop our sense of worth and anchor our individual ego in our body, and, eventually in the world. He wants our light to shine and to help make the world a better place for humanity. He encourages us to be our best and, always, honor ourselves.

Archangel Uriel helps us form stronger levels of self-worth, self-respect, self-esteem, self-confidence, empowerment and freedom. This happens through the challenges and experiences we have in life.

Uriel works from deep within this chakra to strengthen and define our sense of personal identity so we know who we are. With this powerful force working within us we are able to develop a healthy and resilient sense of ourselves. We take this knowing out into the world to give back our talents and define ourselves.

A healthy, viable ego is connected to the spirit and, at the same time, has the capacity to negotiate in the world. Archangel Uriel shows us how to contain the duality of our divine nature and human self with dignity and balance. When we know who we are we also know what we are capable of doing and what will serve our growth and inner development.

Our human side survives by learning to stand up and interface with the world, in the best way that expresses our needs. The more experience we get in being our own advocate for life the easier it becomes and the more confident we are.

Our divine self must turn inward from time to time to refresh itself, touch base with the core foundation of Self that carries the divine God qualities we claim for ourselves. Turning to our divinity allows us to be the loving beings we truly are. We always need to be reminded of our own divine identity. The irony is that this keeps us more human.

Our divinity has an authority that is stronger and far greater than the voice of the world. It always will honor the love, grace and power of God moving in us, living as us. In meditation we feel this force and honor it.

The Solar Plexus Chakra is lit by the majestic spiritual fires of the Archangel Uriel. He brings us our authentic authority and teaches us to stand in our power. He is a great warrior who fuels this chakra with the grace of right action, a ferocious fearlessness that is unafraid.

In meeting our challenges and facing our initiations we strengthen the I AM principle; we fortify what is bold, true and strong in us. In the initiation into the Solar Plexus awakening no one is spared conflicts, fights, or challenges. These are part of building a strong and powerful ego that keeps our forces clear, defined and in the service of the Creator. It teaches us how to manage power with love, compassion and truth.

What the great angelic forces do is to stand with us in meeting our challenges. They help us in the fight, supply us with energy, and teach us to cultivate a wonderful and wholesome sense of ourselves and those who are our enemies. They are helping us define ourselves. We can forgive others and be grateful to them for the role they assumed for our inner development.

Uriel encourages us to find humor in our endeavors and allow our heart to be tender and caring through this period of our development. As we move forward in life the angels cheer us on. They encourage us to be strong and fight the good fight, for love, victory and the glory of God.

MEDITATION ON THE SOLAR PLEXUS

Sit comfortably. Relax and take several deep breaths. As you scan your body, release any areas of tension with your breath. As you breathe in love and power, feel the Divine Presence awakened within you. As you exhale release fear, doubt and confusion. Feel your foundational strength that affirms you and says "YES" to life.

Now find the place within where you have the experience of who you are. No one can touch or strip you of this awareness of yourself. It is where you know, within yourself, your own I AM. Once you have encountered this place you have made a true and indelible connection with God within yourself. This is you, this is Source.

Tell yourself fear has no place in your life and you can meet all your challenges with grace and grit. Release this affirmation as you breathe in and out. Let the Solar Plexus be filled with the light of God living in you, as you and through you.

Repeat to yourself:

I am free, I am worthy.
I am responsible for my life.

Repeat this to yourself:

God is my source. In Him all things are possible.

Feel yourself supported by the great spiritual forces of the Solar Plexus working within you. Their prayer is that you will experience this truth.

Beloved Archangel Uriel, help me build an energetic body that fully contains my strength and protects my sense of worth. Teach me to meet my adversaries with certainty, clear boundaries and with love. Give me clarity and courage to do what I need to do. I am willing and able to meet my challenges with detachment and to follow my guidance and truth. Help me to stay steady, be strong and flexible, and accept that I am always worthy and whole.

AFFIRMATION

I stand in the truth that I am a powerful force
for good.

Angels of the Solar Plexus

The Angel of Self-Worth

The Angel of Self-Worth reminds us we are always worthy of all we hope for and desire. It resides deep within our being and expresses itself through the power of the Solar Plexus Chakra. It helps us affirm our worth whenever we are in doubt about our value. It helps us honor our longing and desire to know love, kindness and respect. It champions the development of our growth, healing and maturity.

This angel teaches us to face our challenges with courage and to stand upright in the face of adversity. It encourages us to look our opposition in the eye and affirm our worth. It serves us as a guide in the realm of personal development so that we become stronger vessels for the Divine Presence to live in and work through.

The Angel of Self-Worth confirms that we are worthy of self-love, self-respect and personal dignity. It always encourages us to fight the good fight, for love, victory and the glory of God and it asks us to be responsible beings.

MEDITATION

Sit quietly. Relax and breathe deeply. Scan your body for tension. Feel if there is any fear lodged in your Solar Plexus Chakra. Be conscious of your Solar Plexus Chakra and sense whether it is contracted and tight or too loose and overly expanded.

As you deepen your breathing allow your chest to expand and your spine to straighten. Feel your legs and the bottoms of your feet on the ground. Be in your body as you continue to monitor your breath. Release tension, fear and uncertainty with a deep, full breath.

Affirm:

> I am here and I am worthy of all I desire
> and want.

Tell yourself:

> I am always manifesting my greatest good
> and everything I need comes to me.

Allow yourself to breathe deeply into your Solar Plexus as you affirm these statements. Know the truth of them within you now.

The Angel of Self-Worth takes you beyond feelings of entitlement to the true understanding of your worth. This allows you to claim your good, knowing you are a beloved child of God and all things come to you because of who you are. Remember that when God is for you no one can be against you.

PRAYER

Beloved Angel of Self-Worth, please stand by me as I face the daunting challenges of life. I choose to be responsible and stand up for myself in life. I want to express my truth and live from the depths of my being. I choose to know my worth and experience my value. I embrace my self-respect and I claim courage, strength and truth. I know this battle for selfhood is a worthy fight. Please help me realize this for my life now.

AFFIRMATION

I am worthy of all that I seek, hope and want.
I accept my worth.

The Angel of Power

Personal power is what we develop as we mature. It allows us to better express what we want and claim for ourselves in life. It can be embraced in a quiet, gentle way but it is power, and power moves things, nevertheless. It is our gift from God and it helps us face the world. The Angel of Power connects us to our power in a conscious way. As we integrate the responsibility of power into our psyche we move towards a balanced and wholesome way of living in the world and being one with God, one with ourselves, and one with others.

The Angel of Power walks the path of power at our side. It guides us carefully, teaching us with wisdom and truth how to engage with others. Power can be soft and quiet. It can embody humor and intelligence. It need not be aggressive or forceful in order to succeed at its tasks. We call our power to us when we claim our good. It is ours to use to express the love, grace and goodness of our being.

MEDITATION

Sit quietly. Relax and take a deep breath. Focus your awareness on your breathing. Take several deep breaths into your Solar Plexus Chakra as you expand the sides of your rib cage. Feel the power of your breath push your chest cavity open. Feel your back expand and your chest fill with air.

As you do breathe in say "YES" to yourself, "YES" to your life, "YES" to your spiritual forces and "YES" to your power. Be willing to recognize the power of love that moves you through the world as a unique expression of your divinity. Power is yours to carry out into the world and a clear definition of who you are. The Angel of Power brings the love, power and healing force of God through you into the world around you. It brings healing to the world and lets you be a beacon for good. Acknowledge this force with gratitude. Use your power to create a wholesome and happy life.

Beloved Angel of Power, please help me accept my power and use it in a loving and wise way. Show me how it serves me to step into my power so I don't fear it and can manage it with grace and love. I want to create my life through the power of my mind to see the good and realize it in all I do. I invoke my power to live a full and happy life. I claim my power to enrich my life and help the world in whatever ways are asked of me. Help me know the power of God's grace working in us all.

I affirm the power of love to heal me
and make me whole.

The Angel of Choice

Choice defines our individuality and is a reflection of our freedom. The Angel of Choice reminds us we always have choice, in every situation we experience. The choice to see the good is ours, as is the choice to be a victim of circumstances. How we choose to experience a situation is a reflection of our growth, maturity and spirituality. Choice is one of the greatest gifts given us by our Creator.

Knowing we can choose love, gratitude and forgiveness gives us power to know ourselves as free beings. It is this power that allows the best of our spirit to shine forth, overcome adversity and claim empowerment for ourselves. We are always free to choose the good.

MEDITATION

Sit quietly. Relax. Breathe deeply and scan your body for tension. Release that tension by breathing deeply into your body. As you breathe into your Solar Plexus Chakra settle into yourself and turn your awareness inward to your deep core.

Allow yourself to choose to be fully in the moment. Affirm your choices for love, light and life to fill your being now. Consciously affirm:

I choose life! I choose love!
I choose to love myself.

As you make choices you call in the angels of healing and love. Conscious choices confirm your desire for a better life and allow it to come to you. Claim your life now and be open to receiving your good, in loving, graceful and elegant ways. Be responsible for the choices you make. Choose what will ultimately make you happy and give you peace.

PRAYER

Beloved Angel of Choice, thank you for helping me choose life and to honor my desire to choose the good. Your guidance supports me in making wise choices for myself and my life. I choose to be happy, fulfilled and grateful. I choose the good, the whole and the loving. Help me be responsible for my choices and to know I am always free to choose the high road.

AFFIRMATION

I choose life, I choose love, I choose my highest good and greatest joy.

CHAPTER 8

The Virtues, Dominions and Dynamis and the Heart Chakra

Just as love is the center of our lives so the Heart Chakra is the center of the human energy system. Its core themes are love, peace and joy. As we allow love into our hearts it heals us and the world around us. It is the truth of our being.

Love radiates from our heart which is the sacred chamber of love, and the temple of the Divine Presence within us. Love transcends the physical, but, at the same time, touches everything in its path. Love opens us, heals us and rejuvenates our spirit. We call it to us and express gratitude for its presence in our lives, however it chooses to manifest in our being.

The heart is the conduit for love to flow through us. It never forgets an act of kindness or moment of love and stores the memories of love deep within its hidden chambers. This is why forgiveness sets the heart free. It releases us from the bondage of anger, hate or enmity. As we heal from the wounds of the heart we release and forgive so we can return to love.

We maintain a healthy heart when we release emotional pain and forgive hurt. As we free ourselves love finds its way to flow as the mighty river it is. It searches out the deep inner caverns of the heart, floods every cell of our being and opens us from the inside out. It permeates our being at the deepest level.

The heart delights in love's lightness, expands in its joy and flourishes in its peace. It dislikes all forms of physical pain and suffering and should be spared anything that will weaken it or make it suffer. It weakens with prolonged grief and the ache of loneliness. The heart must feel the flow of love to be fulfilled no matter how that is expressed. Love recognizes itself only in love.

Love and gratitude comprise the two central themes of the Heart Chakra. They kindle the heart and generate feelings of warmth, tenderness and joy. As we develop into spiritual beings capable of unconditional love we respect the power and wisdom of the heart. It knows when it is full, when it can give and when it must find rest and peace.

Doing what makes the heart sing is a valuable life lesson. When we follow our heart we learn the power of love to move us beyond the powers of reason. We learn what heals the heart and gives life meaning. It is always love, in one form or another.

The Virtues, Dominions and Dynamis

The Heart Chakra is governed by three angelic forces: the Virtues, Dominions and Dynamis. Their task entails keeping the portals of the heart open so love can flow. It takes the entire force of these three angelic beings to work in the Heaven of Creation. They are the guardians of love and their task is to keep the heart strong, expressive and alive in the flow of love.

The Virtues bring us the beauty, and grace of love itself. They embrace us with love. They bring the gift of freedom and choice to help sustain our faith in love. We can only love in freedom. There is no other way to love. It is a free act on our part to love.

These angelic beings work within us to keep the heart resilient, warding off despair, depression and suffering when our spirits are low. They remind us that we have always done our best to bring love into the arena of our life. They help us forget the hurts and wounds. They encourage us to cultivate a belief in ease.

They bring us the wonder of love. They ask us to remember it for the times we feel far from its source. They prepare our spirit to accept love and bring us new experiences of it in our ordinary, daily life. They keep us laughing when times are challenging because we remember love. They remind us we are always watched over and blessed by the great spiritual forces who are love itself.

The Dominions, also known as the Powers, bring the power of peace, harmony and serenity. They act as guardians of the soul and protect the heart from withering when love seems far from our experience. They shield the heart from the pain of rejection, betrayal and neglect. They keep us moving forward after painful loss and hurt.

They help maintain peace as a constant stabilizing force within us. When situations challenge our inner stability these angelic beings remind us to stay the course, practice our meditation, read uplifting books, do our exercises, release our worst fear, and pray for grace.

The Dynamis are the angels who create serenity in our lives. They bestow the gifts of fulfillment and happiness that tell us we have let love into our heart. They keep our spirit calm and grateful for the experience of love. They remind us to choose love and let it live within us. As we create this intention to claim love it becomes easier to allow it into our being. They offer us the choice to love as recourse from the tension and stress of daily life.

The Angels of the Virtues

The Virtues bring us love, freedom and faith. They transform our desires into reality. Every time a dream of love manifests in our hearts it develops more faith that we can receive our good. The Virtues tell us all things are possible, at any age, any time, any place. We just want to be open to love.

The Virtues ask us to trust God's wisdom for the experiences we have that make us clear about our choices for love. They teach us we are worthy of asking for what we want, no matter how impossible it may appear. They help us put our intentions towards the fulfillment of love.

The Virtues sanction us co-creating our lives with God. They know our spiritual evolution intensifies each time we claim our good. They want us to fully experience love and self-empowerment through calling to us that which we want and desire.

The Virtues are a testament to the fact that faith moves mountains. They share in the joy of dreams come true. They delight in our happiness and encourage us to envision continuously all that we want and desire. There is nothing that we cannot create in our life. If we are love then it is love that we will call to us.

The angels of the Virtues are:

The Angel of the Dream

Our dreams embody all our longings and desires. They hold the promise of love, intimacy and spiritual connection as possibilities to be fulfilled. By allowing our dreams the time and space to unfold we gain clarity about what we want and give them the opportunity to manifest.

Love, happiness, abundance, health and wholeness are all aspects of God. They have been bequeathed to us by the Divine as part of our spiritual heritage. Claiming them is how our dreams come to fulfillment. We back up our dreams with faith that they will manifest.

MEDITATION

Sit quietly, relax and take several deep breaths. Scan your body for areas of tension. Breathe into those areas and release the tension.

Begin this meditation by reflecting on something you truly want in your life now. Hold the image of what you desire as if it had already manifested. Feel that sense of satisfaction you claim for yourself now. Experience in your body, feel it in your heart, see it in your inner eye. Know it is real. Give thanks for the power of your dream that has allowed you to claim your good now. The more you imbue your dream with feeling the stronger that vision becomes.

PRAYER

Beloved Angel of the Dream, you hold the power of my heart to realize my deepest longing for love. Please know I long for my dreams of love to come true now. Please help me have the courage to dream the unrealized dreams of love, peace and goodness manifesting as the experience of my life. Know all things come from God and that even the impossible can manifest with faith and trust.

AFFIRMATION

I affirm the power of my dreams to
open my heart to love.

The Angel of Positive Intentionality

Intentionality is focus and clarity of mind, heart and body to claim a desired outcome. It draws to us that which we long for. It is a major component for manifesting our dreams into reality. It clearly tells the universe what it is we want in our lives now.

Positive intention brings together all our forces for envisioning our life. It works to align our feelings and desires with our hopes for our highest good and greatest joy. Intention lets us consciously claim that which we want and know it is manifesting with each positive thought.

MEDITATION

Sit quietly, relax and take several deep breaths. Scan your body for areas of tension. Breathe into these areas and release the tension.

Begin this meditation with pencil and paper at hand. List five intentions for your happiness that you would like now. They may be intentions for love, prosperity, health, happiness and wholeness. Whatever they are, reflect on them, say "yes" to them, accept your desire for them as real. Now write them down. Be as specific as you can about what you want to experience. Know your intention as whole and complete as you offer it to God and release it into the universe. Allow your heart to speak to you about what you truly want to have in your life and claim it now.

Always write your intentions in the first person, stating the word "I." Keep your wording positive and affirmative. Remember, the universe only says yes. Make sure your intentions hold the fullness of your desires. Examples of clear intentions are: "I receive the love I ask for now," or "I have a wonderful new job that respects my talents, honors me and is fun."

PRAYER

Beloved Angel of Positive Intentionality, help me consciously co-create my life now. This intention comes from the best for me. I want to draw into my life that which will bring me happiness health, love and joy. I recognize God as the Source of all things and my intention states clearly what my desires are.

AFFIRMATION

I allow my intentions to yield the good I seek.

The Angel of Faith

The Angel of Faith lives in our hearts to remind us faith can move mountains. It is the essential ingredient for our hopes and dreams to manifest. We need to know that which we claim is manifesting in our life. Faith tells us we have the power to receive our good. It reminds us that our good is here now. Faith sees us through the challenges and reminds us that we are all God's children, capable of co-creating the good for our lives, and free to make choices for love.

Faith is the belief in something hoped for and the knowledge that it will come to us. Faith carries us through the deserts and out of the shadows into life. It is through faith that we are able to reach the far shore of our desires and hopes. Faith gives us courage to move ahead. It helps us take risks and defines what we long for and claim for ourselves.

MEDITATION

Sit comfortably, relax and breathe deeply. Scan your body for areas of tension. Breathe into those areas and release the tension with your breath. Allow yourself to sit quietly and go deep within your heart. Take a big breath and release tension from your heart. Here you will find the core of your faith. Have faith in your Creator to see you through, have faith in God's angels to bless your life in countless ways, have faith in yourself and in life. Have faith that you are carried on the wings of angels and you can meet all the challenges and initiations you face. Allow faith to be your guiding light.

Beloved Angel of Faith, help me remain faithful to
my hopes and dreams, even when I am bruised and
disappointed. Let me have faith that what I seek
and long for is coming into my life. I trust God, love
my life and honor the Divine Presence and I have
faith in my goodness coming to me.

I know that faith will always lead me to higher
ground. I know that in faith I will be carried
forward. Whenever I falter please remind me to
remain faithful. Thank you for your faith in me.

A F F I R M A T I O N

I have faith in the goodness of life.

The Angels of the Dominions

The angels of the Dominions are the Angels of Joy, Forgiveness
and Gratitude. These three angels work together to unleash our
unexpressed life force, and our creativity. When we forgive we
release the grip of resentment and free up our vitality for ease and
pleasure. When we are grateful our whole life expresses thanks to
the Divine Presence that lives in us, as us and through us.
Gratitude is a key component in opening our hearts and feeling
the joy of life.

Joy itself lives at the core of our being. It may be buried under
a mountain of pain, stress and guilt but once we start the healing

process then joy finds its way out from under the morass of limited thoughts and asks us to step up to our lives. Joy becomes the matrix of how we want to live as a moment-by-moment, daily expression of our being. It wants to radiate out into the ethers and touch all life. Joy becomes a determining factor in our choices, our habits and our actions. It defines what we want to feel at the end of a working day, after a conversation with a good friend, and in the arms of someone we love. Joy needs to be cultivated and it takes a determined heart to find it each day, little by little, until we have a repertory of it. Was it in the cloud formations, in your garden, at the grocery store, in a child's voice, in that little moment of rest you gave yourself? It is asking to be cultivated and deeply experienced.

The Angel of Joy

The Angel of Joy resides deep within the heart. It delights in the rhythmical beat of the heart, and flourishes with each moment that joy expressed itself. It honors the cycles and rhythms of the day, the flow of the week, the waxing and waning of the moon. It loves the changes of the seasons, the equinoxes and solstices that mark the year. It finds joy in the ordinary cycles of time that define our lives, each marked by joy.

This angel loves the festivals when joy is always expressed. The Angel of Joy reminds us of the glory of creation. In order to be brilliant and shine its light upon us it rests quietly within us until the appropriate time for expression. It thrives on meditation and stillness, and enjoys the presence of peace and tranquility.

Joy is the antidote to the darkness and heaviness of despair and depression. It releases the burdens of our heart and brings in fresh energy and new light. It helps us raise our expression of gratitude and love to a higher level. It charges the heart forces to be strong and to meet the formidable challenges of life with valor. Reserves of joy keep our heart resilient. It is worthy of cultivation on a daily basis.

Sit quietly. Relax and take several deep breaths. Scan your heart for tension and fears and release them with your breath. Assess your heart to see if it feels contracted or congested. Listen to the beat of your heart, hear the steady sound of it beating. Feel it pumping your life force through your body.

Breathe into your heart and fill it with joy. Now find a memory of love that you cherish. Allow yourself to feel the joy of it. Let your memories fill you with joy. Be thankful for this experience and hold it close to you. Let it remind you life is beautiful and you are free to always remember the joy of it.

PRAYER

Beloved Angel of Joy, open my heart to joy! Help me laugh at my shortcomings and release me from being overly serious about insignificant problems. Help me find joy in small and simple things. Support my daily practice of seeing joy in the world around me. Teach me to laugh, be happy and, please, fill my heart with joy.

I choose joy ! joy! Joy!

The Angel of Gratitude

Allow gratitude to fill your heart with a sense of plenty and abundance. It brings release from disappointment and helps you to forget. Gratitude sets our spirit free and reminds us of the good we have in our life now. It helps us appreciate and honor life and to be grateful for it. It recognizes that there is good in all things and helps us see every experience as a blessing.

Gratitude makes life easier and lighter. It eases the spirit of heavy burdens and it allows the spirit to soar high in appreciation for the good. When we are grateful we affirm who we are and we affirm life itself. An attitude of gratitude opens the doors of our heart so it can receive more.

MEDITATION

Sit quietly. Relax and take several deep breaths. Scan your body for areas of tension as you breathe in and let it go with your exhalation.

Try this meditation at the end of the day. Begin by reflecting on your day. Go over encounters and meetings, conversations, and experiences. Bless each experience with gratitude and release it to spirit.

Cultivating this practice helps release any vestiges of negativity you may have picked up in the day. It sets you free to find healing in sleep and to awaken refreshed, and ready to meet your good.

Beloved Angel of Gratitude, thank you for my life; for all the good and what I considered bad, that I have experienced. Thank you for the challenges which tested my patience, engaged my will and made me stronger. I am grateful for the fortitude it took to get through those challenging times. I am grateful for the strength, wholeness, and maturity I have cultivated and I am grateful for the good I see all around me. Thank you for all I experience, and all that I am.

I am grateful for each moment of life.

The Angel of Forgiveness

Forgiveness releases our heart from the burdens of negativity. It sets the spirit free and opens the heart, once again, to love freely. Forgiveness lets life resume its natural flow. It frees us from the charge of energy that negativity locks into our heart. With each act of forgiveness we become more enlivened, more receptive and better able to enjoy love when it comes into our experience. Forgiveness ends victimhood by allowing love to flow again.

Forgiveness is currency for the soul. Without it we would accumulate so many negative experiences we would crumble under the weight we carry. We would suffer most by not being able to feel love fully. Our channels would be clogged with anger, negativity and stubbornness. We forgive for the sake of love.

Sit quietly, relax and take several deep, full breaths. Scan your body for areas of tension. Breathe into them and release the tension with your breath.

As you go over your day, ask yourself who needs forgiving today. Bring up their names and say in your heart, "I forgive you. I release you. I thank you. I love you. And I bless you." This is a good practice to do as often as you need to for any negative sentiments that linger in your mind. After each encounter feel your heart lighten up. You will experience freedom and enjoy the possibilities of love.

PRAYER

Beloved Angel of Forgiveness, please help me release my negativity and anger. My heart is heavy with the burden of holding it. It weighs me down and dampens my spirit. I want to feel the doors of my heart fly open in joy and the promise of love. I want to receive and give love again. Let me accept life just as it is, being grateful for the experiences I had. Please help me be free to step into the now, ready to love again.

AFFIRMATION

I forgive all those who have hurt me and I especially forgive myself.

The Angels of the Dynamis

The Dynamis bring humanity the spirit of mercy. They influence us by helping us forget and release the past. They inspire both conscious forgetting and conscious remembering to keep us safely living in the arms of love. They rekindle our spirits when we are lost and unsure and bless us with God's mercy.

The Dynamis mend the heart by healing the hurts of the past. They do this through forgetting and remembering. They release blocks to spiritual development by diverting our mind from pain. They bring us into the here and now as we let go of resentment, anger and doubt.

The Dynamis eradicate suffering and remorse from our psyches. They keep the heart pure and innocent so that it can receive its good and go forward into life, receptive to good. They coax us towards the light of love and help us feel safe in its glow. They abide deep within the Heart Chakra, bringing healing and wholeness to the spirit.

The Angel of Release and Letting Go

The Angel of Release and Letting Go helps us to consciously release and let go of all that is unlike love. Through its gracious love we are able to let go of suffering and hardship, and find our way back into life. This angel encourages us to remember love and empty our minds of the burdens of the past. It knows the heart longs to feel light. It is always eager to be joyful and to feel love.

One of the main functions of this angel is to release emotional pain. It helps us free the heart and mind of anger and hatred, knowing these corrode the spirit and weigh down the heart with pain. In order for this angel to thrive in our heart center we must be willing to let go, divest ourselves of worries and burdens and let love into our hearts.

MEDITATION

Sit comfortably, relax, take several deep breaths. Scan your body for areas of tension. Breathe into those areas and release your tension.

As you exhale, release suffering and negativity. Literally blow it out of your mouth. Be willing to let go of hurt, grief, and suffering. Your heart no longer wants to hold onto that pain. It longs to be soft and to feel love and peace, joy and ease. Help it along by your willingness to release your pain and let it go. It no longer serves you. Be merciful to yourself and redeem love.

Do this exercise daily, morning and night, for several weeks and feel your heart lighten. Each step forward is a step to releasing the burdens and suffering of the past. Let go and allow your heart to melt into love.

PRAYER

Beloved Angel of Release, please help me clear and release whatever stands in the way of love coming to me. I pray I can let go of all that weighs my spirit down and holds me back from love. I want to welcome love into my life. I ask to be released of pain, suffering and, especially, self-doubt which make me feel unworthy of love. I long to know the joys of love again and to express it fully. I pray to be able to love again.

I let go of anything that is unlike love. I open myself
to the joy and peace of love.

The Angel of Remembering

The Angel of Remembering floods our psyche with positive
memories of love and moments of nurturing when we experienced the grace of love living in us. This angel kindles the
wonderful memories of love we hold in our heart throughout our
life. It gives us memories we can access when we want to be
reminded of love. As we honor our memories our spirit feels
renewed and lightens up.

Memories of love soften our heart and make us grateful for
what we experienced. They allow us to ask for more. Loving
memories are sacred to the soul because they contain the energy
of love. We can draw upon them at any time we need to
remember love.

MEDITATION

Sit comfortably, relax and take several deep breaths.
Scan your body for areas of tension. Breathe deeply into
them and release the tension.

As you relax allow yourself to go back into your past
memories of people who you loved, cared for and spent
time with. Remember the times you experienced being
loved and carried in the arms of love. Choose a memory
you cherish. Allow it to fill your heart with joy. Give
thanks for it and allow it to soften your heart. These

memories are great treasures for the soul and keep our spirit strong.

Beloved Angel of Remembering, remind me of the wonderful occasions when I experienced love; shared my soul with another being. I know that those were moments when I was held in the arms of love. Help me honor those moments and be grateful for them. Let me draw upon them whenever I need to remember. I hold them as true treasures in my heart.

I honor the memories of love which remind me that I am loveable. I am thankful to all who shared their love with me.

The Angel of Forgetting

The Angel of Forgetting removes memories of pain and hurt from our heart. It helps us forget times of suffering and the moments of torment, worry and grief. It erases anything that ever diminished us, weakened us or hurt us. It sets us free to love ourselves anew and for love to flow in our hearts.

The Angel of Forgetting erases memories of challenging and dissonant times. It eradicates moments we were unhappy or hurt, afraid or overwhelmed by loss. Its function is to protect our heart from pain. We need this as much as we need to remember times of love.

Forgetting is like going to sleep after a challenging day. We awaken refreshed, forgetting the stress of yesterday. We need this forgetting to keep us sane and whole when pain can be overwhelming and we feel our heart is breaking. It is a gift from the angels.

MEDITATION

Sit quietly, relax and take several deep breaths. Release any tension you feel in your body.

Consciously forget past pain and struggle. Allow it to be erased from your memory. Choose to live in the moment and be willing to forget times of discord or sorrow that plague your memory. The past does not serve you now nor does it allow love to find you. Stay open to love as you release the past from your consciousness. Bless it and set it free. Allow the Angel of Forgetting to ease your mind and bring you peace.

PRAYER

Beloved Angel of Forgetting, erase my pain and help me forget my past struggles, and all hurts and sorrows that dampened my spirit. I am resilient and whole today in my forgetting about the past. I consciously choose to forget the times of pain and sorrow. I want to be open to all the joys love can bring to me now. Please keep my mind open and let me forget what hurt me. I ask to live in the now, free to receive love's blessings. Thank you for this great gift of forgetting. I am so grateful for this gift from God. It sets me free and helps me claim my good now.

AFFIRMATION

I release all memories that block my
awareness of love.

The Archangel Raphael and
the Heart Chakra

The Archangel Raphael provides humanity with the healing love of God. He is the archangel God asks to deliver the gift of healing to all. Archangel Raphael rules over the Heart Chakra. He is often depicted holding the great Book of Life. This book contains all the plants used for healing. It contains a list of their medicinal properties.

The biblical legend tells us that Archangel Raphael healed the prophet Tobias's father of blindness. He told Tobias to mix a salve from the ash of burned fish liver and rub it on his father's eyes. When this was done, the old man regained his sight.

He is often portrayed with the caduceus in his hands, the universal symbol of healing. He brings humanity healing at all levels of its being. He wants us whole on the physical, emotional, mental and spiritual levels. His hope is that we live in the fullness of God's love.

We petition him when we need healing in our lives. His ability to regulate the Heart Chakra keeps it open and flowing with love. He helps keep our spirits in balance and he is the great protector of our heart forces.

He brings the gift of regeneration and renewal after illness or trauma. He instills the power of love in us all to be expressed through every medium, and released into the world as healing and regeneration. He brings the force of life to us.

MEDITATION

Sit comfortably, relax and take several deep breaths. Scan your body for areas of tension. Breathe into those areas and release the tension.

Reflect on your health. Ask for what you need to feel balanced and whole within yourself. You can ask for physical healing, emotional healing and mental healing from this great archangel who brings us God's healing love. You can ask for all that you want and long for that will let you feel fulfilled. It all comes from God. If you need healing offer up your prayers, ask directly for what you need. Be blessed.

PRAYER

Beloved Archangel Raphael, you bring healing to earth. Please watch over us. Bless us with good health, protect us from illness. I pray to keep my spirits strong and my body healthy and resilient. Support me with all that I need to be fully present

in my life. I ask for stamina, courage and abundant
love to see me through these demanding times.
Guide me to make good choices for my life.

I am whole and complete through the love of God.
I enjoy perfect health.

CHAPTER 9

The Seraphim and the Throat Chakra

The Throat Chakra is called the Mouth of God in Metaphysics. It is the point where our consciousness is articulated, defined and genuinely responsible for sharing the depths of our being with God, the angels and our fellow travelers on the path of life. It is through the power of speech that we offer up our petitions to God and speak our truth to others.

As our Throat Chakra releases all the suppression that a lifetime of constriction, compliance and conformity has demanded of us, it begins to form a band of solid integrity around it. Self-expression takes form, we heal from the grief of not being able to express our authentic self and begin to live in the truth of our being. As we mend we develop a richer capacity to speak our truth and allow our inner light to express itself.

The powerful forces of the Seraphim work within the Throat Chakra under the guidance of the Archangel Gabriel, who brings us the Word of God. They work to infuse us with integrity, and a strong and powerful will. They help us become someone who clearly speaks and understands the truth, and who shares clear communication with others. Living and expressing ourselves creatively is the outcome of having a strong Throat Chakra.

The Throat Chakra sits within the throat and supplies energy to the mouth, tongue, teeth, neck, external and internal throat and the ears. The qualities of the Throat Chakra are: clear communication, creativity, willpower, truth and our personal integrity.

These qualities define an individuated person; someone who can hear and follow their inner guidance and who is able to express their truth with love, clarity and compassion. This person listens to his inner guidance when angels whisper in their ears. They know the value of truth and are always living in integrity with themselves.

The chakra sits very close to the exterior of the throat. It is delicate and susceptible, especially when we are tired, emotionally suppressed or unhappy. There is a fine balance between self-awareness and self-expression that is reflected in this chakra. It is also susceptible to substance abuse, as addictive substances tend to pass through the throat. Because the quality of will sits within this chakra it needs to be fortified and strong to withstand toxic substances which weaken the physical fiber of the throat.

These are the qualities of the Throat Chakra:

Integrity and Truth

The Throat Chakra is a high spiritual center. It requires that we live in alignment and resonance with our spirit. This means living in our integrity, expressing our truth and being honest with others.

The Throat Chakra is weakened by the toxicity of negative speech, lying, malicious gossip and substance abuse. All addictions pass through the narrow passage of the throat. Smoking, drugs, medications and over- and undereating affect this chakra. As people come into the time of life when this chakra develops, from 28 to 36, they will rethink the diversions that keep their truth suppressed. Then they can easily develop these inner qualities for their spiritual life.

The Throat Chakra is the bridge between the feelings of the heart and the thoughts of the mind. It expands and strengthens our expression of the truth and it gives us power to be our authentic self with others. It contracts when we suppress our feelings or lie. We control our energy through our thoughts and actions as well as our words.

Creativity

The Throat Chakra is the center of creativity. In the modern world truth has been the victim of suppression. For people who have not expressed themselves authentically it takes great fortitude and courage to heal their Throat Chakra. We can begin to open this center through expressing ourselves through creative media such as singing, painting, music, dance or the infinite variety of ways we can showcase our unique and special self. Creativity is an avenue to higher consciousness.

Communication

We learn to express our feelings and share our truths with others through the power of speech. Clear communication reflects the best of our ability to share ourselves. It reflects emotional maturity and a level of detachment from embarrassment or timidity that stands in the way of sharing ourselves.

The more clearly we speak our truth, express our needs and

open the door for dialogue, the more clearly our spirit expresses itself through us. We become the channel for higher spiritual forces to work through us. Angels can whisper in our ears and give us our guidance. Communication with higher powers is as simple as it is with those around us.

Willpower

Will is our volition in action. We want to create a strong will that can withstand temptation. The will is the strongest part of our nature. Will is sacred and honors the way in which we have formed our individuality. It protects us from giving our selves away, it strengthens our ability to do the tasks at hand, and it supplies us with the strength and focus in the face of complexity that requires thinking and forethought.

Will can be formed through acts of self-discipline. If the spirit is to be strong and discerning it wants a sense of self-mastery. Will strengthens our resolve to see something through to the end. It allows us to trust in ourselves and know we are capable, and able to persevere in life. As we awaken to the inner truth of our strength we also cultivate this important center.

The Seraphim and the Throat Chakra

The Seraphim are the first of the angelic beings abiding in the Heaven of Paradise. They are also known as the angels of miracles. They assist God in creating those synchronistic moments, when destiny and fate meet one another and good happens. We call such moments miracles.

181

They align with our intentions for the highest good to unfold. They create opportunities for healing and love to flow in and through us. They remind us that there is a far higher power than our small, edited ego, working within the universe for the good of all.

The Seraphim help us harness our will forces. They keep us stable during change and keep us from losing ourselves in enthrallments and diversions. They open our minds to endless new ideas which release the realm of possibilities into the world of manifestation when we choose something we want in our life.

The Seraphim allow our good to flow in the direction of cure, bringing with it happiness, health, prosperity and joy. They give us strength to move forward regardless of circumstances. Their hope is that we will develop our integrity.

They teach us to value our word, express our truth and honor God as Source. They encourage us to communicate our deepest feelings and longings. They want us to love fully and without censure, and to live without fear.

Their task is to help us live our best life. In order for that to come about they want us to speak our highest truth about what we want, what we feel and how we hope to live our life from the highest and best place we can imagine. They know the truth of us better than we do. They know what is hidden, buried, and needs to come forward in the light of freedom. They wait for us to tire of lying to ourselves about our needs, desires and hopes, and be in truth about our deepest longing and desires. The Angels of the Seraphim are:

The Angel of Will

Will is our volition in action. It is our strongest life-affirming force. Without will we might easily give up, retire from life and wither away. With our will we move forward, strive for excellence, pursue new avenues of learning and development.

We can focus our will in our physical activities, like athletes and performers do; we can use it for our emotional control and impulse regulation, which may be required to withstand challenges and obstacles; we can use it in our mental development to learn something new, or move into a new area of study or expertise.

Our will is fortified and strengthened by angelic forces that work within us. They want us to develop a strong will and use it appropriately. Will marks us as individuals responsible for what we do and what we say. Will informs the choices we make about what we want in life.

It takes a strong will to be positive and affirming in all circumstances. It goes against the common, collective belief that we are not good enough to have what we want. Will says we shall accomplish our striving for empowerment, personal growth and healing. It asserts that we will be positive, capable and responsible advocates for the good.

Will is developed through trials and challenges. It is directly linked to the I AM principle that defines the soul's nature. Will is a signature of our ability to stand upright, speak our truth, and live in freedom, regardless of external circumstances.

MEDITATION

Sit quietly, relax and take several deep breaths. Scan your body for areas of tension. Breathe into those areas to release that tension.

Focus your awareness in your throat, neck, or jaw. Pay attention to the tension around these areas that have accumulated from stress and tension. See if you can release this tension by applying your will to letting go in this area. As you release any tension in these areas be mindful you are using your will to do this.

Now that you have used your will to create a desired outcome be still and listen to your inner voice. See if you can let it reach your awareness. Listen to what is being communicated to you by the wise guidance of your life. Allow the angels to whisper loving thoughts in your ears. They want you to know how much they love and value you. What do you hear?

Practice this exercise of letting go of your tension. When you feel relaxed listen to your guidance. Use your will to create the perfect opportunity for love and healing to come to you.

PRAYER

Beloved Angel of Will, strengthen my will so I may walk in integrity and face my challenges with grace. Help me focus on using my will to defend my right to joy, goodness and love in my life. I ask for perseverance and determination to sustain my will on behalf of my good. I ask your support for this. Thank you.

AFFIRMATION

I affirm my right to express my truth.

The Angel of Integrity

Integrity means whole and integrated. We are whole and at one with ourselves when we live in the truth of who we are. Integrity is also the ethical code by which we live and communicate the truth of our being with others. It means we tell our truth, no matter how uncomfortable we are about it. We do what we say we are going to do. Integrity honors our being. It guides our lives towards a higher meaning and helps us find happiness, health, and bliss.

People with integrity "walk their talk," and are constant and reliable. Integrity reflects character and suggests high levels of self-esteem. Integrity is the mark of a good, true and loving person.

Without integrity in a relationship there is no trust. It is an important quality suggesting a person has inner strength and moral fiber. Integrity develops as we live out our lives. We learn to value it in ourselves and in others. We are not born with it. We cultivate it.

MEDITATION

Be quiet, relax and take several deep breaths. Scan your body for areas of tension. Release those places with your breath.

Become quiet, look inward and reflect on your levels of integrity. Ask yourself if you can improve your own integrity. Are you a person others see as trustworthy, reliable and honest? Can you be counted on to speak your truth? Can you be counted on to do your best for yourself and for others? Can you be counted on to

185

show up when someone needs you? Can you tell yourself the truth about what is important to you?

If you need help in this area call on the Angel of Integrity to help you. We are all working to strengthen our levels of integrity and live more conscious lives.

PRAYER

Dearest Angel of Integrity, help me to be responsible and accountable for my words and for my actions. Let me always do what I say I will do so others can count on me as trustworthy and reliable. Teach me to live in complete integrity with myself so I honor my own needs, and express my dreams and hopes and serve the higher good. I ask your support in developing a firm grip on reality so my integrity can shine in the world and carry me through to a higher level of service.

AFFIRMATION

I stand in my integrity.
I honor the truth of my being.

The Angel of Miracles

Miracles are an ordinary event for angels, and extraordinary for humanity. We think of them as major occurrences, but, in truth, they are part of the "job description" for angels. A miracle brings us the unexpected. It opens the doors of our minds to the power of God to make anything happen. It cuts right through our hopelessness and despair.

The miracle of life engages our hearts and heals our spirit. Miracles remind us that we, ourselves, are miracles in God's eyes. We can't possibly make a miracle happen. It comes as a wonderful surprise, out of the blue, and lets us say "thank you" to life for something unexpected and deeply desired.

Miracles flow easily from the arms of grace. They enhance our lives, surprise us totally and are a gift from God. Miracles keep us faithful in His ever-present love. They heal and transform our lives.

MEDITATION

Sit quietly, relax, take several deep breaths. Scan your body for areas of tension. Use your breath to release those areas. As you turn your consciousness inward reflect on your life. Can you see the miracle of love, truth and light working as you? You are a miracle. As you accept the truth of this, look into the small, daily miracles of love that fortify you. Be willing to see that you are a prayer answered for someone and a gift to life itself.

PRAYER

Beloved Angel of Miracles, thank you for the miracle of my life. I am grateful for who I am, living the life I love. Thank you for my existence, and for giving me the miracle of life. I acknowledge that my life is a divine miracle. I offer thanks.

AFFIRMATION

I am open to and receptive to miracles.

Archangel Gabriel and the Throat Chakra

The Archangel Gabriel rules the Throat Chakra. He brings us the Word of God. Archangel Gabriel is also known as the Bearer of The Word. He appeared to the Blessed Virgin Mary to tell her she would bear a Savior to the world. He reminds us God's Word holds the power to create.

Archangel Gabriel appears in Old Testament stories. In the Koran he is the angel who took the Prophet to heaven one starry night to learn the cosmic truths that became a code of inspired teaching for an entire nation. Within it are contained wholeness, unity and truth.

The Archangel Gabriel teaches us to live in truth. He asks us to open our hearts, listen to our divine guidance and inner wisdom. He helps us hold the silence within so we can hear God. Out of the silence angels bring revelations, inspiration and awareness.

We honor the Archangel Gabriel during the Holy Nights of Christmas. His holy day is 29 December. He brings inspiration and creativity to each soul and awakens the Holy Child within each of us. He releases the gift of the Holy Spirit to give birth to acts and deeds of love and wholeness that transform the world.

We call on the Archangel Gabriel to open our hearts and heal our Throat Chakra. He helps us speak out, tell our truth and sing our song. He reminds us we are all Holy children of God, held in love and honored for our unique contribution to life.

MEDITATION

Sit quietly, relax, take several deep breaths. Scan your body for areas of tension. Breathe into those areas and release the tension.

As you begin this meditation open your heart, throat and mind to the power of Archangel Gabriel acting through you. Feel that you can receive the Word of God and be guided in your life to greater consciousness, deeper truths and beautiful expressions of yourself.

You can express yourself in many ways. You can draw, paint, write, move or dance. Find a way to share your creative gifts. You will feel enriched doing so.

PRAYER

Beloved Archangel Gabriel, please guide me to speak my truth clearly, openly and with love. Help me communicate my needs for love, kindness and respect to all whom I meet and engage with. I know the truth of my spirit is love. I wish to express this in my words, deeds and actions. Guide me to live as a holy expression of the power of the Word.

AFFIRMATION

I live the creative expression of God speaking through me, living as me and moving in me.

CHAPTER 10

The Cherubim and the Brow Chakra

The Brow Chakra is called the control center because it governs our physical health, emotional stability and mental clarity. Its qualities are: the cultivation of wisdom, the accumulation of knowledge, and the ability to discern who and what is for our highest good. It is the center for intuition and imagination.

The Brow Chakra is ruled by the Cherubim who are the angelic forces of wisdom. The Goddess symbolizes this wisdom because it is considered to come from the feminine aspect of God. The Cherubim exist in the Heaven of Paradise and sit close to God. They are often pictured with large wings filled with hundreds of eyes because they are all-seeing and all-knowing.

The primary function of the Brow Chakra is to create intelligence and detachment. This keeps us from becoming too fiercely engaged in any situation where we become enmeshed or entangled. The Brow Chakra energy helps us to think about situations and problems with clarity and vision. Being able to discern the issues we are dealing with helps us stay free and disengaged from emotional turmoil and unhealthy entanglements.

The Brow Chakra serves us in all situations where we are required to think about ourselves, and decide what is the best course of action for us. It gives us the clarity and presence to think how we are going to implement our goals so we can achieve success. We want and need a sharp mind to see us through life's decisions. Learning to think takes a combination of detachment and wisdom.

We can ask the Cherubim to guide us in making wholesome choices for our life. We know that our ability to think clearly defines the best use of our intelligence and they are gifted at helping with that. We may not always be on the mark with our thinking but we are headed in the right direction when we look carefully and assess the reality of the situation for ourselves.

The power of the Brow Chakra is in being able to discern, gather knowledge, distill wisdom and access intuitive knowing. It is always playing chess with life, looking for new opportunities, making shifts in our internal perception, changing from one tack to another. Sometimes asking for wise guidance in our life is the best way to gather a sense of whether something is right for us or not.

Wisdom

Wisdom comes out of being able to distill good from the challenges of our lives. We can also tap into the accumulated wisdom of the collective found in the holy scriptures of all races. There is wisdom to be found in listening to our bodies and in looking at the patterns of our lives. They will all give accurate information about wisdom if we can but listen. Wisdom reminds us that each experience we have makes us stronger vessels for God's love. Wisdom is more valuable than gold.

Knowledge

Knowledge is the accumulated wisdom of the collective unconscious that gives information about how to live one's life. It has been established over lifetimes of exploration, discovery, and involvement in the physical, psychological and mental worlds. Knowledge helps us to live our lives in a better way. It gives us guidance and understanding that help us determine a positive course of action. It can help us decide our path.

Intuition

This is a powerful tool for knowing the truth of ourselves and any situation we are involved in. Our inner guidance system is based on our ability to listen to our intuition. It informs our being about any circumstance or situation we need clarity about. Intuition is defined as the ability to access our deepest knowing and understanding of the truth.

Imagination

Imagination is our ability to see an internal picture of what we want for ourselves. It creates the picture of the life we want. It is developed from actively visualizing what we want to manifest in our experience. This can include seeing a house, car, or money in the bank. It is a gift from the divine to help us create our life the way we would like it to be.

Discernment

This is defined as our ability to know who and what is for our highest good. Discernment is a viable tool for filtering out what does not serve our happiness, fulfillment or growth. It helps us make wise choices about who and what works in our lives. It lets us know we are on the right path to love and true connections.

The Cherubim and the Brow Chakra

These are the angelic forces that bring compassion, intuition and knowledge to the higher mind. They are also known as the Spirits of Harmony. They are ruled by Isis–Sophia, the great goddess of wisdom, and the Shekinah, known in Judaism as the feminine face of God. They bring us insight and clarity. They help us see the light in all situations where we are unsure of our purpose or confused as to which fork of the path to follow.

They work closely with mankind during periods of transition and change. They channel the higher vibrations of wisdom and clarity into the mind. They do this by stimulating the hearts and minds of those capable of receiving their wisdom. They channel this gift of consciousness to us and we claim it as our own bright idea. They are only interested in bringing healing to mankind and the planet and flood our minds with ideas, thoughts, songs, and even poems.

On a personal level the Cherubim provide us with the wisdom we need to help us live healthy and enriched lives. They inspire our thoughts and, ultimately, influence our actions. They always work through the astral body directly into our minds. They want us to be clear vessels of truth, creativity and love.

They help us tap into the depths of our ancestral wisdom that bring the qualities of simplicity, steadfastness and kindness. They remind us, in this complex age, that life is simple. Many new healing techniques come directly from their inspiration.

One of the greatest gifts they provide us with is serenity and harmony. They help us find a way to be at peace with ourselves and to accept that whatever has befallen us leads us to our good. They show us how to access our inner resources through the power of thought and they help us transform the negative ideas and attitudes we harbor. They reveal the laws of the universe to us which give us the higher truth, unconditional love, and complete freedom we need to live conscious lives. They remind us we are loved beyond measure.

The angels of the Cherubim are:

The Angel of Wisdom

The Bible says that wisdom is more valuable than gold. It is stored within us as repositories of consciousness that come out of the hardships, suffering and abuse of the collective unconscious.

The Angel of Wisdom enlightens our minds that there is only one life, and one truth, and that is God. They tell us that life is always perfect, just the way it is. They help us to accept the truth and find the wisdom we need that will sustain us through our trials and initiations into love.

Ancient wisdom honors prayer, gives value to meditation, and appreciates quiet reflection. These are ways of accessing our inner guidance. We can tap into the pools of the collective wisdom whenever we need answers in our lives. They are there to be known.

Having access to this wisdom helps us make good choices and points the way to how we want our future to look. This wisdom wants to be known and asks to be experienced. It has accumulated from trial and error over lifetimes.

It is this distillation of collective wisdom that teaches us the laws of peace, patience, right action, emotional trust and loyalty. If we allow ourselves to experience wisdom we will know true power and create our lives in a good way. It only asks to be recognized.

MEDITATION

Sit quietly, relax and take several deep breaths. Scan your body for tension. Breathe into that tension and release it.

Turn your awareness inward to your Brow Chakra, located between your eyebrows. This is known as the Third Eye. It refers to the ability to "see" the truth. It is the pathway to intuition, knowledge and wisdom. If you have a question regarding a choice you would like to make and you want to access your wise guidance ask your angels for wisdom regarding this situation.

Find love and comfort in your inner wisdom. It can guide you through perilous times and also bring you great inner peace. When you listen carefully you will hear that all is well. Let this ease your fears. It will set you free and allow you to be responsible for the choices you make.

Beloved Angel of Wisdom, help me tap into the
depths of my knowing. Show me how I can honor
the wise guidance of my life. I choose to live in the
truth that my guidance knows exactly what I need.
Please support me in making wholesome choices for
my good. Let love always guide my path and move
me forward.

I trust the wise guidance of my life. It always shows
me the way forward.

The Angel of the Law

The Angel of the Law represents the eternal structure that holds
the universe together. These laws are immutable. They are based
on God's love and mercy for His creation and they govern all life.

They are, in fact, what we call the moral impulse that helps
people know right from wrong. It is systemically and organically
programmed into all life unless some impediment blocks that
from occurring. We are all subject to the conditions of this law
which define us as creatures of love, light and infinite possibility.
When we claim our good we come to understand that it is all
revealed to us through law.

The law defines our spiritual growth and inner development
and it gives back to us what we claim for ourselves. It takes us
from one archetype of empowerment to the next through the

medium of consciousness. It teaches us to do good and love unconditionally and that, in doing so, we will receive that which we give out.

In law there are no victims, only clear reflections of levels of consciousness that give us what we have given out. When we claim our good it is that which we receive from law. When we claim other than good, that is what will be given.

The law treats us as we treat ourselves. When we begin to love ourselves and enhance our self-esteem the law will manifest higher levels of love and situations where we are replete in our self-esteem.

The law is benign. It does not punish, it does not harm. We do those things to ourselves. The law is blessed by God's mercy. It invites us to give, to care for others, and to be a part of the human community. It encourages us to do good in whatever ways we can and, always, to be at peace knowing that the love we have given is ours to claim for ourselves.

MEDITATION

Sit quietly, relax, and take several deep breaths. Scan your body for areas of tension. Breathe into those areas to release your tension.

Begin this meditation by considering how law works in your life. Law gives you exactly what you believe to be true about yourself. What are the beliefs you hold on to to reflect your sense of worthiness? If you are willing to release old, worn ideas and re-form better ones about yourself, the law will reflect your new thinking. Create beliefs about your power, beauty and intelligence that make you worthy of what you claim for yourself. Claim

love, life, and joy for yourself now. Ask the angels to open
your heart to allow you to receive what you want in your
life. Let law do the rest.

Beloved Angel of the Law, help me accept my value
and know I am worthy of love, kindness and respect.
I claim happiness, love, prosperity, health and joy
for my life now. I take responsibility for what I
choose and I allow law to manifest itself now by
fulfilling what I claim. I release all thoughts that
define me as separate, unworthy or not enough. I
release all beliefs about punishment, struggle and
toil that diminish me.

I claim my good now in love and joy.

AFFIRMATION

I claim my good now. I abide in love.

The Angel of Eternity

The Angel of Eternity reminds us we have forever to complete
our spiritual journey. Earth is the teaching planet where we learn
the higher truths about the nature of love and unconditional forgiveness. It is where we have the opportunity to experience
ourselves as whole and complete, capable of living in freedom
and finding happiness.

Our spirit is eternal. It lives forever through lifetimes. It is programmed, in each life, to work through self-limiting beliefs, challenges and suffering to come to know the soul's eternal worth and expand its consciousness of God.

As we love ourselves more we come closer to the realization that we are always whole and complete. In this knowing we allow life to express the joys and goodness we claim for ourselves now. Life gives us the opportunity to know the truth of who we are and to bring heaven to earth to enjoy that.

It takes only a moment to know our worth. Accepting that we are good, whole, beautiful, worthy of all we say we want completes us. It also allows us to claim our good.

MEDITATION

Sit quietly, relax and take several deep breaths. Scan your body for areas of tension. Release that tension with your breath.

Take a moment to acknowledge: "My spirit is eternal." Listen carefully to your words as you take them into your heart. They can free you from any sense of urgency that you have to be right and perfect all the time. Growth implies periods of awkwardness, and the uncomfortable feelings when we are beginning to experiment with new ways of being. When we allow ourselves to grow from spiritual infants to mature adults in God we must walk every step in the truth of what is revealed to us at the moment. Release ideas that you must be "perfect" to experience happiness and wholeness. It is yours now if you claim it. As you accept more and more of your good it becomes familiar and easier at each step of the way.

Beloved Angel of Eternity, help me know, in the depth of my being, that my spirit is eternal. I have chosen numerous forms and endless experiences that have defined my being over a lifetime. Now I choose love, wholeness and joy. I claim my happiness in this lifetime. I rejoice in knowing it is mine now. Help me live each moment in the grace of this eternal truth.

AFFIRMATION

I affirm that my spirit is eternal. It never is born and it never dies.

The Great Goddesses and the Brow Chakra

The Brow Chakra is governed by the feminine forces of the Shekinah, or the feminine face of God, and Isis–Sophia, Goddess of Divine Wisdom. The feminine is receptive and embodies the beauty, truth and elegance of the goddess. She becomes an archetype we can recognize and integrate within us when we seek to cultivate wisdom in our lives.

The Goddess includes all aspects of our soul's journey, including the shadow. It accepts us for who we are, both at a divine manifestation and a very human level of being. She accepts us as we are, without trying to change or alter our human nature. She gives us the intelligence to transform what has been wounded and damaged in ourselves through the power of love. She wants us to better enjoy and love our lives.

The goddess knows the truth of all situations, and honors spirit as a living reality within each person. She is rich in love and compassion, and brings peace that heals to all mankind. The feminine principal embraces the truth of our inner wisdom and values kindness, love and beauty as intrinsic qualities in all interactions between people. She recognizes each individual as whole and free at all times to choose their good.

The Goddess stimulates right thinking about the serious issues plaguing humanity. She opens the channel through which divine ideas stream into the consciousness of mankind. She offers us the possibility of healing our wounded souls and leaves that choice to us.

Her attitudes are rich in wisdom and she brings a living consciousness that honors all life forms. She helps us become free from fear, struggle and toil as we come to accept and love ourselves. She frees us from punishment, judgment and hurt. She helps us find intuitive solutions that emanate from the spirit and bring welcome solutions to the world.

The Goddess directs wisdom directly into our minds through the Third Eye. This mixes the forces of love with a deeper, richer, and more expanded consciousness that will serve humanity and improve quality of life.

She encourages us to seek creative solutions and gentle ways to move forward. She supports our conscious evolution and validates our self-love and wholeness. She does not punish, or hurt, but, rather, encourages us to strive for what is wholesome and natural, choosing a better way forward.

Her influence is as old as life; her wisdom ancient. She is aligned with the forces of the moon and the power of angels to bring the feminine and receptive into our thinking, feeling and willing. The Brow Chakra is subject to weakness by over-mechanization, over-calculation and evidence-based measurable results. It is depleted of its natural gifts of intuition, imagination and creativity. When we cultivate these and integrate them they support our capacity for visionary thinking. They bring the Goddess alive in the world.

The Goddess

Being conscious of the powerful feminine energy of the Goddess creates a vortex around us that channels angelic love, divine blessings and direct guidance into our minds. These enter our consciousness and serve to guide us with ease through the challenges of life. We are blessed to recognize the Goddess working in our lives. She is the counterforce to all that is active, aggressive, mathematical and mechanical. She brings us rest, beauty, darkness and the opportunity to heal.

She carries us through travail, chaos and disharmony. She tempers our will forces and slows us down so we can smell the roses and experience the goodness around us. She reminds us of the importance of family, children, and home, good food, healthy boundaries, holidays, rituals and festivals.

She brings peace when we are agitated and helps us accept ourselves just as we are. She brings play, theatre and comedy into our experience. She is moist, full of life and beautiful. She reminds us there is always another day to fight the good fight for love, victory and the glory of God. Her suggestion would be to relax and enjoy ourselves for a while before we get back into the fray. She is rich in humor, delights in jest and sees the forces of life as positive, joyful and wholesome.

Sit quietly, relax, and take several deep breaths. Scan your body for areas of tension. Release that tension with your breath.

As you sit in meditation reflect on the power of your mind and how you use it for your good. Do you fill it with information or do you seek knowledge and wisdom about the higher truths of life? You have the choice to think thoughts that support your happiness or ones that punish and belittle your spirit.

Can you find joy and ease in self-acceptance, love for yourself, appreciation for your life just as it is? This is the power of the Shekinah and Isis–Sophia. These goddesses let you know you are a gift to the world. They encourage you to think loving, good thoughts about yourself.

PRAYER

Beloved Shekinah, Isis–Sophia, loving Goddess, help me to transform my thinking to be more spontaneous, joyful and humorous. Help me learn to play this game called life and win the prize of happiness, fulfillment, joy and creativity. Help me be more receptive to the world of spirit, and honor the truths that define my life. Help me find time for ease, pleasure, and love. Let them flow effortlessly in my life. Teach me to stop the struggle and relax. Thank you.

AFFIRMATION

I transform my thinking to include the best
and loveliest I can imagine. I allow my wisdom
to come forth.

CHAPTER 11

The Thrones and the Crown Chakra

The Crown Chakra is the highest energy point in the human energy system. It holds a highly refined energy and a field that carries the spiritual dimensions of our life within it. We can be assured that as we develop internal awareness and become spiritual the Crown Chakra acts as a radiant beacon of light to the spiritual world.

The Thrones are the angelic beings who rule the Crown Chakra. They sit at the highest tier of the Heaven of Paradise and are believed to reside at the throne of God singing His praise and glory. They include the Angel of the Holy Spirit and the Angel of the Christ Light amongst them.

The Thrones transform our limited understanding of reality into an expanded awareness of how God works within each of us, blessing us with love, healing and mercy. The Thrones are known as the Eyes of God. They gaze deeply into the truth of our being, know our strengths and weaknesses and our spiritual path. They are able to support us in moving through what is old, dank, and unloving in our consciousness.

They live in the present moment of time, which is always eternal. They are perpetually honoring the majesty of God. They have a powerful influence on humanity because of their radiance and joy.

The Thrones help us fulfill our spiritual contracts that we agreed upon while still inhabiting the spirit realm. These contracts, designed to expand our awareness and release old karmic patterns that enmeshed us for lifetimes, enlighten us as to the nature of compassion, love and healing. They help us transform what has previously been outside of the realms of reconciliation.

The deepest wounds of separation are now possible to heal at this level of consciousness. They remind us that nothing about our character or our relationships is written in stone. We have all come to heal. The Thrones remind us that we can make our lives and the lives of those we meet easier and happier through love.

They assist us in our spiritual development by directly creating circumstances that bring us to the awareness of truth, love and healing. How we implement those qualities in our life and relationships is always our choice. We can make it fun and creative, serious or challenging, but the task of reconciliation is ours to do, none the less.

At the end of our life the Thrones will guide our spirit home to God. They teach us death is a simple transition for the spirit, which is eternal. They will ask us if we accomplished our task of bringing healing.

The Thrones remind us the spirit has no limitation. It lives forever; it never dies and is never born. They hope we can live in the truth of spirit at all times. They encourage us to know we are always free to choose our path and that life is benign. The fears we have and sense of separation we carry are ours to overcome and lay aside.

The Thrones bring us the grace and mercy of the Almighty.

Without this to ease our way in life we would experience constant suffering and disappointment. We need the help of the entire angelic realm to progress on our path. This is orchestrated by the Thrones.

They bring humanity healing at all levels and regeneration as the gift of being in a physical body. We can experience them in times of transition, and when people come into our lives and go out.

The Thrones guide our spiritual re-education. They work with us in reprogramming old ideas that limit the self and make it dependent on external evidence for its sense of value and worth. We need their assistance in letting go of our preconceived ideas about ourselves so that we can better love and honor the truth of ourselves.

The Thrones and the Crown Chakra

The Crown Chakra is the last chakra on the ascending scale in the human energy system. It sits at the top of the head and opens at age 42. It evolves until age 49 when our awareness expands sufficiently to include the great mysteries and we are on our path towards spiritual development and internal healing. This is a time when spirit points us towards our destiny and opens the doors to inner development and awareness.

The Crown Chakra is the repository of our soul forces. It contains the Christ Light and the essence of the Holy Spirit; both powerful spiritual forces that teach us the power of healing and the essence of love. They are aspects of the Divine Presence living within us. They carry the power of reconciliation, healing, and grace for our lives.

When we awaken to our spirituality we can follow the path that brought us to the recognition of spirit. We can see how we have been guided through many circumstances, and many people, to take the next step on our path. When we awaken the Crown Chakra we live with a spiritualized consciousness about our life and the circumstances and choices others make as well.

The Crown Chakra opens to receive direct guidance from the angelic realm, the Christ Light and the Holy Spirit. When we are guided the mystery of life unfolds before us and we follow a path of light, wonder and mystery. It contains all the energy we need to live a conscious, happy and intentional life. It is sustained by our indelible link to God as Source. It is the link to spirit through our prayers, petitions, visions and hopes. At this level we know all that we need is provided for us and that we are blessed in endless ways that fulfill our life.

This link to God can never be broken or destroyed. It can, however, be weakened by focusing too intently on the material world or by negative thoughts and actions. Conversely, it can be strengthened through meditation, prayer, forgiveness and gratitude.

The qualities of the Crown Chakra are: bliss, beauty and serenity.

Bliss

This is the highest state we can achieve and still remain in our body. It is often called enlightenment as we have a direct experience of who we are. It is a perfect state of peace, acceptance and compassion. In this state there is no craving, no anger, no desire, no fear. It is the eternal now. In it we have the experience of complete oneness with all life.

Bliss is the inner space where we are untouched by the mundane and still carry out our daily tasks. We live our lives in the moment and respond with love rather than reactivity when we are challenged. We cultivate love, compassion and truth, and we are co-creating our future in a reality of wholeness.

Beauty

Beauty is the shining light of our soul emanating through to the world around us. Beauty couples warmth of spirit with the qualities of love, peace and serenity. It is never a well-made, cold object but something that is permeated with spirit. It is an experience of grace manifesting in form. It contains within it a feeling, a vision or an object made with love. The angels only see beauty and potential in people.

To the ancients beauty was considered a virtue. It enabled people to forget, momentarily, their mundane existence and see the higher good and reflection of God. Beauty is a metaphor for the inner truth of our being.

Serenity

This is a state of quietness that combines the joy of harmony and the peace of tranquility. It is an inner place that reflects our highest truths, deep abiding love for the self and compassion for others. It implies absolute acceptance of what is. It has a fragrance of its own that is a rare perfume that calms our senses and assuages our appetites. Serenity is a goal worth cultivating in the disquiet of our busy life. Serenity is a spiritual quality. it holds the world steady, and keeps our tasks proportional to our capacities. It is never reactive nor overbearing. It is a state of mind that soothes, heals and sustains.

The Angel of Bliss

The Angel of Bliss holds our hearts in its wings. It creates the space within us where we live in the grace of God, through the trials and challenges of daily life. This bliss is the blessing of the Christ Light and the Holy Spirit. It tells us that we are blessed and our lives are transformed through grace. We know, at the heart of all things, that all is well, regardless of how they seem to appear. We no longer become hooked into the dramas and enmeshments that create frustration or anger. We fully accept life as a miracle.

When we feel blessed we release control and let God move us. We allow a higher power than our limited mind to support us and take care of us. We always receive what we need, in perfect ways, at the right time. When we acknowledge the higher purpose of our lives we begin to walk the path of destiny. In this awareness everything we need comes to us, be it money, love, people, or healing.

MEDITATION

Sit quietly, relax and take several deep breaths. Scan your body for areas of tension. Breathe into those areas and release that tension.

210

Take a moment to reflect on your passion for life. Have you ever met teachers, doctors, healers, parents, hard workers, or simply wonderful people who live a passionate life? They love their life and what they do. They are happy and content with how things unfold in their lives. This passion is palpable. It takes commitment, wisdom and love to keep that flame burning.

Do you want to experience bliss? Are you willing to live your life in that state now? Are you willing to surrender control of how you think your life must be? Can you allow the Holy Spirit to direct your life, and bring you all that you need? Your work is to have sufficient trust and substantial faith coupled with the deep experience that you are loved to allow this to unfold.

PRAYER

Beloved Angel of Bliss, open the doors of my higher mind and let the Christ Light flood my spirit. I am open to receiving the blessings of the Holy Spirit as I move along my path in life. I thank you for the miracle of life and I surrender to your love, truth and beauty now. Let me live in this awareness of truth. Please inspire me, fill me with joy and accept my gratitude for life now. I know this is my bliss.

AFFIRMATION

I choose to follow my bliss and live it fully.

The Angel of Beauty

Beauty is intrinsic to our being. It is a quality that comes from God and when we live out of our deepest connection with life we are beautiful regardless of what the external manifestations appear to be. Beauty is who we are as much as freedom, wholeness and truth are who we are.

As we acknowledge the truth of our being, our inner beauty radiates out to the world. Beauty is not about our physicality as much as it is a reflection of our essence. If we give it room to express itself as us, as we allow freedom, wholeness and truth to live from our experience, it will heal our self-hatred, and sense of inadequacy and unworthiness.

Beauty is a reflection of our soul. When we let our light shine it manifests in the world around us. It reveals itself in our bodies, in our gardens, and homes. It is simply a clear expression of who we are.

MEDITATION

Sit quietly, relax, and take several deep breaths. Scan your body for areas of tension. Breathe into those areas and release your tension.

Think of a beautiful place that stands out in your mind. It can be the ocean, a park, a garden, a baby or anything that touched your soul with its beauty. Remember the feeling you experienced when you witnessed beauty. It works within you and touches the place where beauty lives within you. It can soften your heart and keep your spirit fueled. Let beauty shine its light on your world.

Oh, Angel of Beauty, thank you for the joy you bring me. My world is richer because of the blessing of beauty. I love a beautiful environment, a beautiful creation, a beautiful soul. I love feeling beauty around me and in me. Thank you for the glory of nature and the beauty of the world you show to me. I rejoice in seeing the beauty in others and I am so grateful.

AFFIRMATION

I live in beauty, I walk in beauty, I breathe in beauty,
I am beauty.

The Angel of Serenity

Serenity brings such delight and happiness. It can relieve our distress and anxiety and iron out the inroads fear makes in our mind. It keeps us internally balanced when we are overloaded with tension. It cuts through toxic thoughts to bring us to a place of inner peace and joy.

Choosing a path of serenity requires a willingness to embrace the highest truth that everything is in perfect order, and God is working in everything, even the chaos we see in the world. It is possible to remain in a serene state when we reflect on the Divine Presence and know we are carried in love by the great spiritual forces of creation.

We can choose serenity as a lifestyle. When we make the

choice for it we ease down and relax. Serenity implies self-acceptance and non-judgment. It gives others the freedom to be themselves. It is a way of saying yes to life, yes to the moment, yes to how it feels, with gratitude and love.

MEDITATION

Sit quietly and relax. Take several deep breaths. Let go of whatever worries you have and be in the experience of living in the moment.

In this moment there is only serenity. There is beauty around you, bliss within you and you feel serene and calm. Nothing can destroy this feeling. You are anchored in your serenity and choose this place, this space when you want rest and peace.

PRAYER

Dear Angel of Serenity, thank you for showing me I can be serene through challenges and change. I choose to cultivate a more serene attitude to life and I ask your help. Please help me release negativity, fear and doubt that drain me of serenity. Help me be confident that all is well. Help me make my world one of harmony, bliss and serenity.

AFFIRMATION

I am serene and calm as I walk the path of life.

The Crown Chakra and the Angels of the Holy Spirit and the Christ Light

The Crown Chakra is the portal through which the Holy Spirit enters our being. It graces us with complete acceptance and unconditional love and it works to heal any sense of separation, isolation and fear we have. It informs our soul that love is forever present and truth is ours for the knowing. We can experience it working in us and influencing our lives.

The Holy Spirit brings us moments of communion, and a sense of holy alliance with those we love. It allows us to bless our enemies, love strangers and know we are always connected to a higher Source of good *no matter what*.

The Holy Spirit works through us, lives as us, and moves in us. As we grow spiritually we know the truth of our being as one in God. We honor God in all things, all people, all places and all creatures. The Holy Spirit is the messenger of God's love, compassion and mercy. It removes pain, eases transitions, transforms the negative into a higher awareness of truth. It heals our soul from any sense of duality.

Through the grace of the Holy Spirit shame, guilt, and errors of judgment are rectified. It reveals the infinite compassion and love of God's true nature to us as a model to follow in our daily lives. It will always show us our own innocence and purity of spirit because that is who we are at our core. It erases what is unwholesome, impure and defiled in us. It never punishes, but only forgives and loves.

The Christ Light is the highest wisdom and truth that lives within us. It is the pure light of Divine love working within us. The Christ Light reveals that we are all children of God, all worthy, all graced and all accepted just as we are.

The Christ Light reveals the power of the Divine working within us to inform our ordinary life that God lives in us, as us as Divine love. As this truth grows within our consciousness we develop into wholesome beings able to live well and trust in life. This light fills our being as it expands into the truth of life. It heals us and opens our hearts to love.

The Christ Light is the purest template of God's love. It lives in our guidance, is our north star, our highest truth. It directs our experience of life to be transformed into the conscious awareness of love. It invites us to be happy, fulfilled and thankful. It expresses through us as loving kindness, creativity and compassion.

The Christ Light exists in all people. It may be called by another name, such as consciousness, Buddha, Atman, or Brahman. It signifies the Self, our highest potential, our indelible connection to Source within.

The Christ Light within us serves as a beacon to the angelic realm that we are growing, learning, absorbing truths, transforming limitation and expanding our Selves. The forces of the angelic realm, who work for our healing and development, delight in seeing our light expand and our wounds heal.

The Angel of the Holy Spirit

The Angel of the Holy Spirit brings God's grace into our field. It holds each soul carefully in its wings and honors each choice we make as a step towards love. It always gives us what we need to temper the soul and strengthen our being.

As we grow and mature we develop the capacity to hold the forces of the Holy Spirit more fully. As we forgive, reconcile and accept ourselves we expand our spiritual nature and embody the

Holy Spirit more and more. Gratitude is what we give back to life for the experience of the Holy Spirit working in us.

The Holy Spirit teaches us that what makes us happy makes God happy. We are not here to sacrifice; to be martyrs dying before we have completed our journey. We are here to find joy and happiness, fulfillment, health and prosperity and live a full life. Allowing the grace of the Holy Spirit to enter our lives sets this path in motion.

MEDITATION

Sit quietly, relax and take several deep breaths. Scan your body for areas of tension. Breathe into those areas and release any tension.

Sit in silence and create a channel between your conscious mind and the Holy Spirit. Call it to you and request its blessing upon your life. Feel its kindness and love. It is pure goodness. Feel its sweetness as your heart melts. Feel your spirit strengthen. The Holy Spirit sees you. It comes because God loves you. It acknowledges your spirit, generosity of heart and capacity for kindness.

Ask the Holy Spirit to bring you what you need to live the life you want. If you need money, ask for it; good friends, ask for them; love and warmth, ask for them. It will all be given. There is no need to struggle or punish yourself by depriving yourself of what you need. Allow God to provide for you with ease, joy, and pleasure what you need to make your life work. It is yours for the asking.

PRAYER

Beloved Angel of the Holy Spirit, thank you for the grace you bring to my life. I wish to be a vessel of Your love, power and healing. I choose to carry the flame of Divine love into the world, express it around me and light the hearts and minds of all those who I meet. I release all doubt and fear. I live in truth and love. Help me ground my gifts, and realize my full potential.

AFFIRMATION

I affirm the power of the Holy Spirit
working in my life now.

The Angel of the Christ Light

As we evolve into mature spiritual beings we realize God illuminates and transposes our lives to higher ground with each challenge we face, each act of love we offer, and each moment we are aware. We unite our consciousness with God as we embody the Angel of the Christ Light.

The Angel of the Christ Light lives within us and strengthens our indelible connection with God. It helps us know the depth and truth of God's love for us. It keeps us grateful and humble. Our spirit grows as we allow the Christ Light to shine its light within us. It opens us to our wholeness, and defines our sense our freedom.

The Christ Light is the Divine Presence of God living within each of us. It was embodied by Jesus of Nazareth, who was a fully enlightened teacher. He lived the power of God within Himself and fully experienced the truth of God within Himself.

He taught us that every person carries this light. As we heal and become conscious we become the light that we are.

MEDITATION

Sit quietly, relax, take several deep breaths. Scan your body for areas of tension. Breathe into those areas and release the tension.

Visualize an angel behind you, in front of you, and on either side of you. Call them in to your meditation. Ask them to bless you and to protect the Christ Light working within you. Feel this energy move through your chakras, opening up your subtle bodies, embrace your soul forces and your spirit. It is so powerful that it can purify your being in an instant. Open yourself now to receiving your good. Allow your wounds to be healed. You are one in God.

Allow the Christ Light to strengthen your body, affirm your worth, and honor your choices for love. As you reflect on this live in the peace and love that it brings you. Know the Christ Light is the living presence within you. It asks to be recognized, embraced and honored in every person you meet. Let that light shine in your heart and radiate out into the world. Choose to honor this light within you.

PRAYER

Beloved Angel of the Christ Light, help me fortify my connection to God through the awareness of the Christ Light within me. Let me bring your love and light to the world in whatever capacity I am able. Heal my soul from the delusion of separation. Help me bring healing, truth and love to all situations in the light of your love.

AFFIRMATION

The Christ Light illuminates my life in all that I do and all that I am.

Conclusion

Be blessed in your life with all that you feel serves your connection with the angelic realm. We have the delusion that we are capable of living our lives by ourselves, without help, without succor, without the sweetness the human spirit is capable of sharing. We need one another, we need to be the angels that we know live in us. Let them manifest as us so that we can bring concrete solutions to our world, so in need of help, so in need of our care.

Angels abound everywhere. They come in the kindness of strangers, the sweet words of friends, the smile from a neighbor. If we are missing that connection with our fellow humans let us make ourselves a little more visible so that the angel within us can shine its light to help others.

Take the truths of this book and make them your own. They come as gifts from the spirit realm, through me, to you. If they can make your world richer and your life happier then angels have touched your lives. We all thank you for reading this book, sharing it with your friends and loved ones.

BIBLIOGRAPHY

Attwater, Donald, *The Penguin Dictionary of Saints*. Harmondsworth, Middlesex, Penguin Books, 1975.

Ben Shimon Halevy, Se'ev, *The Divine Plan*, San Francisco, Harper San Francisco, 1996.

Boros, Ladislau, *Angels and Men*, Search Press, 1974.

Brandon, S.D.F. (ed.), *A Dictionary of Comparative Religion*, New York, Charles Scribner & Sons, 1970.

Burnhan, Sophie, *A Book of Angels*, New York, Ballantine Books, 1990.

Connolly, David, *In Search of Angels*, New York, Putnam Publishing, 1993.

Cross, F.L. (ed.), *The Oxford Dictionary of the Christian Church*, London, Oxford University Press, 1966.

Davidson, Gustav, *A Dictionary of Angels*, New York, The Free Press, 1967.

Mallasz, Gita, *Talking with Angels*, Einsiedeln, Switzerland, Daimon Verlag, 1992.

Moolenburgh, H.C., *A Handbook of Angels*, Saffron Walden, Essex, C.W. Daniel, 1988.

Steiner, Rudolf, *The Spiritual Hierarchies*, New York, Anthroposophical Press, 1970.

Steiner, Rudolf, *Angel*, London, The Rudolf Steiner Press, 1996.

Synnestvedt, Sig, *The Essential Swedenborg*, New York, The Swedenborg Foundation, 1970.

Szekely, Edmond Bordeaux, *The Gospel of the Essenes*, Saffron Walden, Essex, C.W. Daniel, 1979.

Wauters, Ambika, *Angel Blessings for Babies*, London, Carroll & Brown Ltd, 2010.

Wauters, Ambika, *The Angel Oracle*, London, Connections Press, Eddison-Sadd Ltd, 1995.

Wauters, Ambika, *The Angelic Year*, London, Carrol & Brown Ltd, 2001.